AUTUMNS IN SHIRE WITH GUN.

BY THE HON. A. E. GATHORNE-HARDY

WITH ILLUSTRATIONS BY
ARCHIBALD THORBURN

SECOND EDITION

LONGMANS, GREEN, AND CO.
39 PATERNOSTER ROW, LONDON
NEW YORK AND BOMBAY   1900

All rights reserved

An improvised drive.

AFFECTIONATELY DEDICATED

TO

JOHN WINGFIELD MALCOLM

FIRST LORD MALCOLM OF POLTALLOCH

PREFACE

MOST of the following sketches were originally published in the *National Review* and the *Badminton Magazine*, and in a special Christmas number of *Rod and Gun*. I desire to thank the publishers of those periodicals for permission to reproduce them in a collected form. I have revised the whole, and added an introductory chapter and a new article; but, while I have omitted repetitions and corrected some mistakes, I have not thought it desirable to rewrite much, as I desire to convey to my readers the fresh impressions produced upon my own mind at the time by various days' sports in the West Highlands.

CONTENTS

CHAPTER I.
	PAGE
POLTALLOCH	1

CHAPTER II.
FALLOW-DEER AT HOME	22

CHAPTER III.
CHASING THE ROE	42

CHAPTER IV.
FIRST IMPRESSIONS OF DEER-STALKING . . .	57

CHAPTER V.
THE HERDS OF PROTEUS	72

CHAPTER VI.
A DAY WITH A SEAL	87

CHAPTER VII.
OUT OF THE DEPTHS	103

CHAPTER VIII.
WESTERN WATERS	136

CONTENTS

CHAPTER IX.
NIL DESPERANDUM 153

CHAPTER X.
A DAY WITH THE GRILSE 163

CHAPTER XI.
LOCH-NA-LARICH 176

CHAPTER XII.
GROUSE 186

CHAPTER XIII.
GROUSE-DRIVING 201

CHAPTER XIV.
CHILL OCTOBER 211

LIST OF ILLUSTRATIONS

AN IMPROVISED DRIVE	*Frontispiece*
WILD-CAT ON THE WATCH	*to face page* 10
THE HAUNT OF THE ROE	,, 42
SOME SHOOTABLE BEASTS	,, 61
A SEAL-HAUNTED ROCK	,, 96
PLENTY OF TIME!	,, 169
A CAPITAL POINT	,, 197
THE OLD RIVER	,, 217

AUTUMNS IN ARGYLESHIRE WITH ROD AND GUN

CHAPTER I

POLTALLOCH

It was in 1846, more than half a century ago, that Charles St. John published his "Wild Sports of the Highlands," a collection of sketches of sport and natural history which still holds the field as one of the masterpieces of sporting literature. If I hope that my random sketches of a later period may prove of some interest, I trust I may be acquitted of the presumption of challenging direct comparison with a classic of such well-merited fame. In addition to the qualifications of unrivalled power of observation, and an easy and luminous style, St. John enjoyed the advantage of a comparatively untrodden field, whereas there are now few indeed of those who care for sport who are not familiar with many parts of the Highlands. Still an experience of more than thirty years, mainly in one district peculiarly favourably situated for the enjoyment of almost every variety of High-

A

land sport, and the study of wild nature in many aspects, may be my justification for submitting my rough sketches to the public in a collected form, and, like my master and model, I ask indulgence for their unfinished style, and for the necessarily copious use of the first person singular. I have jotted down from time to time these personal reminiscences of various kinds of sport as typical, not of extraordinary successes, but of fairly normal experiences; and as they were generally written down while the facts were fresh in my memory, they may, I trust, be relied upon as accurate. Perhaps they may awake pleasant recollections in the minds of some who have enjoyed the same healthy and restful relaxation in the great playground of the British race.

It is difficult for those who receive the annual influx of agents' circulars offering every description of Highland sport and accommodation, to realise the changes that have come over the Highlands during the century now drawing to its close. If Walter Scott, the pioneer of picturesque Scotland, were recalled to life, he would hardly recognise more than the external natural landmarks of many of the scenes which he described so well. The open hospitality which, in his time, made every casual visitor to the village inn or manse free to range hill or river-side after stag, muirfowl, or salmon, of course became impracticable when improved means of communication sent a vast invading army annually northward. But the wholesale system of letting sporting rights is of comparatively recent introduction, and great changes have come about even within my own experience of little more than a generation. The moor where, in 1872, four guns, of whom I was one, killed over 1500 brace of grouse between the 12th and 24th of August in ten "lawful days," was then let with a most commodious lodge and a nice stretch of fishing for £600 a year. Mr. Aflalo, in his work on the cost of sport, still adheres to the rough estimate of £1 for each brace of grouse as the probable cost of sporting rights,[1] including lodge accommodation; but although I hesitate to differ from so high an authority, I should prefer to fix the figure at something much nearer a pound a bird, and good fishing rents have certainly more than doubled in amount in the last twenty years. It is, however, only fair to proprietors to admit that the requirements of tenants in respect of house accommodation, furniture, and sanitary arrangements have greatly increased, and that a very large proportion of the apparent increase of rent represents interest on outlay necessitated by such demands. Formerly the annual visit to the Highlands was looked upon as a sort of picnic or campaign, of which "roughing it" was

---

[1] Mr. Aflalo is not personally responsible for this opinion. He edited the work on the "Cost of Sport," and the statement referred to comes in a signed article by Mr. Teesdale Buckle.

one of the pleasures; and visitors cheerfully submitted to be doubled up in attics and garrets at which the very servants would turn up their noses in these more effeminate days. Rats swarmed about the basements of many of the old ramshackle buildings, and did not scruple to penetrate on occasions into the sitting-rooms and bedrooms. I have a vivid recollection of one particular night in Ross-shire, when a great rat got accidentally shut up in my bedroom, and kept running round and round, passing on each occasion over my face as I lay in bed. Half-awake and half-asleep after a hard day on the hill, I was too lazy to get up, but felt a grim satisfaction when a splash and a scraping announced that my tormentor had fallen into my hip-bath. I had, however, hardly got to sleep again before my enemy made his escape and resumed his rounds, dragging his now "moist, unpleasant body" over my face as before. Whether he left off or I ceased to heed him and fell asleep, I cannot say, but in the early morning I saw him endeavouring to hide on the top shelf of a cupboard where a lot of chintz, pin-cushions, and miscellaneous rubbish, had been put away by the former occupants. I jumped up and locked the cupboard door, and flattered myself that I had secured my revenge for the morning, when I summoned my brother to assist in the execution of the intruder. Armed with poker and stick, we cautiously opened the door of the hiding-place, but had hardly commenced the search when the rat jumped on to my shoulder and down on to the floor, and after a brief chase and a few ineffectual blows vanished up the chimney. I thought we had seen the last of him, but later in the day he emerged, damp and sooty, from the fireplace of another room where the housemaid was cleaning up; and a footman, attracted by her screams, came to the rescue and made an end of him.

Deer forests have not appreciated in value to the same extent as grouse-moors and salmon-rivers. There are various reasons for this difference, among which may be noted the shortness of the stalking season and the heavy expenses connected with the sport; but I think the fact is principally attributable to the hospitable instincts of would-be tenants of sporting rights. Many of these take places mainly with the view of entertaining their friends; and a grouse-moor, especially one suited for driving, is more likely to give the greatest happiness for the greatest number, than a forest where many thousands of acres are necessary to provide sport for two rifles a day. However, any sort of barren moorland is now a gold-mine to many a needy laird, and the same caution should be observed in the investigation of the alluring advertisements of agencies as in testing the *bona fides* and accuracy of prospectus-mongers and promoters. *Caveat emptor* is the rule, and the description of the adventures of Mr. Brixey and Mr. Fribbles in the

"Tommiebeg shootings" is hardly an exaggeration of the deceits and allurements occasionally practised upon the tyro by a low class of agents, while even the most scrupulous must of necessity rely largely on hearsay information. The best advice an old hand can give to those who intend to take a moor is, that they should put themselves, if possible, in direct communication with some former tenant before making an offer; and never conclude a bargain without personal inspection.

My first acquaintance with Scotland was made in the year 1867, when my lucky star took me to Poltalloch, the beautiful property of the Malcolms, just opposite the Crinan Canal. From that date until the present year I have spent every autumn in Scotland, and most of them at the sportsman's paradise where I paid my first visit to the North, and, as nearly all the subsequent sketches describe incidents which took place there, I must briefly describe its geographical situation and characteristics.

Poltalloch comprises upwards of 100,000 acres of moorland and plantations, interspersed with arable and pasture land in the straths and glens. It extends southward along the Sound of Jura to the mouth of Loch Sween in Cantyre, and is bounded on the west by Loch Crinan and Loch Craignish, extending northward and eastward along the shores of Loch Awe. Questions of political economy are foreign to my subject, but it is permissible to allude to the magnificent roads which owe their existence to three generations of owners of this great estate, and to the extensive draining operations which have created the greater part of the arable and pasture land in the glens. Those who inveigh against "unearned increment" should recollect, that there is another side of the question: and I have often heard the late laird announce his readiness to hand over his Scotch property to any one who would repay the capital expended on permanent improvements without any interest whatever. Of course, he would have done nothing of the kind; and I can imagine his face if any one had closed with his offer; but I have little doubt that, from a purely financial point of view, the bargain would have been an excellent one for the seller. His father, who drained the Crinan moss, kept elaborate accounts of the expense of the operation, and only destroyed them in a fit of temper when he found that he had spent more money on his hobby than would have purchased the fee-simple of an equal acreage of the best land in Lincolnshire in its prosperous days; but, although he destroyed the records of his expenditure, he continued his operations to the bitter end.

A naturalist and sportsman may be permitted to regret the utilitarian proceeding which turned the greater part of an ideal snipe bog into indifferent farms. Especially do I owe a grudge to the deep drains through which the rain hurries to the river, instead of soaking gradually through the spongy peat moss. The little salmon river rises and falls in consequence with indecent precipitation; and it has often been my lot to be flooded out on one day, and after a fine night to find the upper pools too low for sport on the following morning. It is owing to the sheep drains that all the Scotch rivers not connected with any large lake now rise and fall too rapidly; but the little Add has a few tidal pools where there is always some chance of a grilse, or a few sea-trout; and it is not often that there is a very prolonged drought in the Western Highlands. I know no species of Highland game, except ptarmigan and capercailzie, which cannot be found within the bounds of the property, although red deer have not penetrated beyond the woods on the shores of Loch Awe. More than a score of lochs provide good trout fishing in the spring and summer, and there is capital sea fishing along the coast, while the marine zoologist finds incomparable dredging ground in the deep and sheltered waters of Loch Craignish, and other beautiful bays and creeks. Opposite the mouth of Loch Crinan lies a long row of rocky islands round which great sport can be had with lythe and saithe at the turn of the tide. Beautiful plumose anemones may be seen here in the clear water, and off one of these islands named Rua is a little natural harbour famous in the early part of the century as the resort of smugglers, who used to run their luggers in behind a low rock, and after taking down their masts, remain perfectly concealed until the coast was clear, when their contraband cargo could be safely unloaded. Smuggling was very common all along the coast in those days of high duties and remunerative prices, and I am afraid the sympathies of the entire neighbourhood from the laird to the crofter were with the "free-traders," and against the constituted authorities. I have often heard the old laird repeat a conversation which took place between his grandfather and the factor. "You will find a hogshead of claret in the cellar," said the latter. "Dear me," replied Poltalloch, "how could it have got there!" "Came on shore in a gale of wind," was the reply; and it was thought as well to ask no further questions.

One species of wild animal, the wild cat, may be taken to have disappeared from the district within living memory. I never saw or heard of one on the estate while I was a resident; but two were killed there not very long before. The last one, a very fine specimen, fell to the gun of the present Lord Malcolm when shooting woodcock in Daltote wood in Cantyre, a plantation of fir trees then not much higher than the knee. The little terriers routing about in the thick cover found something unusual, and the particular one who took credit for the discovery could hardly be prevailed upon to leave the bearer of the body of his quarry after it had been deposited in the game-bag, but followed him about as much as to say, "That is my cat." The bag that day was a varied one, as a jack snipe, a woodcock, a roebuck, and a wild cat fell to four successive shots. Mr. Egremont Lascelles, while watching for deer near the woods by Loch Craignish, had a long shot with the rifle at another, as it crossed the steep brae at the back of Ormaig farm. It was trapped very shortly afterwards, and proved to be a true wild cat. Fifty years ago, according to Brodie, the old keeper, there were a good many upon the estate, and he told me that he had taken as large a number as six in the course of one visit to his traps between Kilmartin and the head of Loch Awe. This interesting creature which, according to Lydekker, has been an inhabitant of Great Britain since the age of the mammoth, would be by this time as extinct as that quadruped but for the deer forests, in the remote recesses of which it still finds a sanctuary. I do not, however, agree with Mr. Lydekker in ascribing its extermination from many of its former haunts to the increased use of fire-arms. Nocturnal in its habits, it cannot often afford a mark for the gun of a sportsman or keeper; but it is very easily trapped, and the enhanced value of moors in the Highlands has naturally led to the destruction of so undesirable a neighbour for game and black-game.

Wild cat on the watch.

A curious adventure with one of these creatures is described by Mr. Alfred Lubbock in his "Memories of Eton and Etonians." He killed this "fine genuine wild stump-tailed cat, *Felix catus*," in 1862, in the forest of Wyvis, near Inverness. He was coming down the river to fish on a very stormy and windy day, when he saw something running along the bank, every now and then stopping and looking as if it wanted to get across the river, but was afraid to jump in and tackle the stream. He threw down his rod and ran after it, picking up two or three stones as he went. Owing to the wind, and the noise of it and of the stream combined, the animal did not seem to hear him until he got within about fifteen yards of it, when it stopped and looked round at him, and he saw that it was a cat. In an instant he "let go one of the stones at it, catching it on the head, and it rolled over." Certainly the occurrence was a most remarkable one; but to those who remember the narrator's accuracy of aim and power of throwing, the fact of his getting a chance at a wild cat will seem more strange than his success in taking advantage of it.

The beautiful little pine marten still makes an occasional appearance in Argyleshire. Two at least have been trapped upon the Poltalloch estate during the last ten years. One was caught there about 1890, and the keeper then told me that the last he had trapped before was caught "the day the new church was opened," which fixes the date as 1853. Another, a bitch that had never had cubs, was caught in Oib Graem, in the rabbit warren, in 1895. Colonel Malcolm of Achnamara, a keen naturalist, greatly regretted that his visitor had met with so inhospitable a reception; but these agile creatures are such great travellers that it would be impossible to preserve them effectually on any single estate, however large. It must, I fear, be admitted to be mischievous and ferocious; St. John describes it as one of the most destructive of its tribe, and says that the shepherds accuse it of destroying great numbers of sheep. "His method of attack is said to be by seizing the unfortunate sheep by the nose, which he eats away until the animal is destroyed on the spot, and dies a lingering death." As he also adds that they kill numbers of lambs; and, when they take to poultry killing, enter the hen-house fearlessly, committing immense havoc, in fact, seldom leaving a single fowl alive, it would not be easy to justify their preservation, or to regret that they have ceased to be as abundant as when he used frequently to shoot them with the rifle on the tall pine trees in Sutherlandshire. They destroy game of all kinds, and even squirrels, and their character altogether is so bad, that one who deprecates the absolute extinction of any of our indigenous fauna will best serve his purpose by dropping the subject.

If some animals are disappearing others are taking their place. It is difficult for one who has often seen the rabbits on a hill-side in the evening swarming like mites in an old Cheshire cheese, to realise that these destructive little creatures were for the first time artificially introduced into Argyleshire by Mr. Askew at Minard Castle in 1845, and that the comments of the neighbours upon the attempt was that it would never do, that the climate was too wet, and that it was no use to attempt to acclimatise a creature so obviously unsuited by nature for the locality. Would that the prophecy had been correct! The rabbits have become almost as great a pest as they are in Australia, and defy the elements everywhere, except along the river banks, where great numbers are drowned by unusually heavy floods, and even there they speedily recruit their numbers, and sport about as merrily and carelessly as others did before the flood in the days of Noe. In Scotland, as elsewhere, they are a source of strife between gamekeepers and tenants; but paradoxically enough it would seem that the former are the advocates of their destruction and the latter of their preservation. Many of the farmers pay a large proportion of their rent out of the profits made from the sale of this spontaneously developed crop, and resent their being trapped or snared by the laird's retainers, while they themselves neglect to keep them down during the early summer months, when they are valueless and unsaleable. On a grouse moor they can only be regarded as an unmitigated nuisance; as it is hardly possible to prevent any but the steadiest dogs from pointing them, while few are shot from the double fear of over-burdening the gillies and spoiling the dogs. Even in covert shooting in the North they give no sport at all commensurate with their numbers, and altogether I thoroughly sympathise with old Brodie, the keeper, who used to tell me that he remembered their first appearance, and wished he had the last pair of them by the neck.

It is difficult to give even an approximate estimate of the number killed annually, but the present head-keeper reports that he and his staff, during the six winter months, October to March, kill 6000 couple on an average. About 200 couple a week are killed about the home farm and woods, and in spite of all this rabbits are increasing. Add to this record the number killed by the farmer, and during the summer months, and it makes the 26,000 which I seem to remember as the number recorded during one year in the '70's, by no means an extravagant estimate. The best sport they give, in my opinion, is as a mark for a pea rifle. It is easy to get rid of a whole pocketful of cartridges during an afternoon's stroll over Benan, and each little separate gully and valley provides one, and often several, chances as you creep over the sky-line. If the wind is strong the slight report of a ·295 cartridge is hardly heard at all, and I have killed as many as eight in one place before a miss sent one off running and gave the alarm to his companions. Only the head or shoulder should be aimed at, as it is distressing to see a badly-hit creature struggle away to die a lingering death in some cairn or hole. One drawback is the carriage of the bag. A keeper or gillie dangling at one's heels is destructive to sport of this kind; yet it is quite easy soon to kill more than most sportsmen would care to carry with them. The best plan is to have an attendant to keep you in sight with instructions to remain at least 200 yards behind, and only follow to gather up the game when you have disappeared over the sky-line.

The fox is, of course, regarded as pure vermin, and even a greater enemy to the farmer than to the game preserver. The number killed at Poltalloch during the three years 1894, 1895, and 1896 were 84, 63, and 75 respectively. 9, 7, and 8 otters, and 3, 4, and 4 badgers were also trapped in the same years. I do not think much trouble is taken to catch these last, and fancy they are still fairly numerous, although their nocturnal habits render them rarely visible to the ordinary visitor to the Highlands. I never myself saw one in a wild state; but this proves nothing, as I only saw foxes on the hills or in the woods on three or four occasions during my autumn rambles on the

West Coast, although they are so numerous as to be a nuisance.

I have never had the good fortune to see the golden eagle on the Poltalloch estate, although I have frequently watched its splendid flight in and near the deer forests farther north. I do not suppose it nests anywhere nearer than the island of Jura, where that excellent sportsman and naturalist, Mr. Henry Evans, forbids their destruction. A pair of ospreys used to build on the old ruined castle of Innischonnell, on Loch Awe, but they were ruthlessly murdered by a tourist who climbed up the old ivied wall, and shot the hen on the nest, and the cock as it returned from a fishing expedition.[1] I have often watched these beautiful birds by another northern loch which shall be nameless, and it is a rare treat to see them soaring over the blue water to their home in the inaccessible precipice where they nest. They do little or no harm, as the fish they take do not materially affect the supply as compared with other destructive agencies, and they certainly ought to be protected legally by the local authorities, and also by the landowners, who should

---

[1] I regret to say this is incorrect. A gentleman who has spent his holidays in Argyleshire for forty years has written to me to say that the hen osprey was shot by the keeper at Eridene, in spite of his protestations. I am sure if it had been known at Poltalloch the keeper would have been sent away. The occurrence took place in 1876 or 1878. My correspondent believes that the cock bird escaped.

instruct their keepers and watchers to prevent the depredations of marauding egg and skin collectors. Four years ago, when it was reported that a fine specimen of a sea eagle had been taken at Sonachan with a trap hanging from one of its talons, my brother-in-law, Lord Malcolm of Poltalloch, telegraphed to buy it, fondly hoping that it was really an osprey which had returned to its old haunt. It proved, however, to be a genuine sea eagle, with a fine appetite for rabbits, which had to be supplied in large quantities during its period of convalescence. The bruised talon was treated successfully by the keeper, and when the patient had quite recovered he was ordered to let him go. " What! " said the keeper, "are you not going to keep him in a cage?" "Certainly not," said Poltalloch, "let him go at once." Accordingly he was taken to Benan, and sailed majestically out with the west wind which was blowing strong, but he must have turned south afterwards, for he spent some time on the Achindarroch estate by the Crinan Canal, where he was unmolested and protected. I can give no account of his movements after he deserted those quarters, but he probably escaped with his life, as I should almost certainly have heard of it had he been shot or trapped.

The eagle owl has been more than once accidentally trapped on the estate, where no owls are intentionally interfered with, and many of the smaller varieties are fairly common. I remember one instance at least of a visit from the Great Snowy Owl. The keeper coming back from Macaskan, an island in Loch Craignish, where he had been after an outlying deer, described to me a large pure white owl which he saw rise from a rock a short distance off the shore, and wing its noiseless flight northwards, pursued and mobbed by terns and gulls. No other bird the least answers to the description of its size, colour, and flight given to me by a fairly accurate observer. Most descriptions of hawks and buzzards are fairly numerous, and none of them except the sparrow-hawk are systematically destroyed. I have watched many an interesting chase of the peregrine after ducks, plovers, curlews, and terns, and of the merlin after his smaller quarry. All the Corvidæ are tolerably common on the mainland, with the exception of the chough, and I have had opportunities of studying the glossy plumage and red beak and legs of that interesting survival on some of the Hebridean Islands, where he was once far commoner than the mischievous and now ubiquitous jackdaw. Sea birds of all kinds abound, and I note with pleasure the increase of the eider-duck, which is now quite a familiar object in most of the sea lochs on the west coast. The young birds when about three-quarter grown are peculiarly helpless; so much so, that if, as occasionally happens, they are left high and dry on shore by the ebb, they wait for the tide to rise again instead of waddling down over the sand. My son, the first time he saw one of these birds stranded in this fashion, knocked it on the head, under the impression that he was putting a wounded bird out of its misery; but subsequent experience has taught us that it is quite a common occurrence, and that it is no physical injury, but mere awkwardness and laziness, which prevents them from waddling over the sand to their native element. Once in the water laziness and awkwardness are both at an end, and the youngest birds can dive and swim strongly and gracefully even where a wild sea is breaking over sunken rocks.

I have frequently had opportunities of watching a rarer visitor, the beautiful little grey phalarope, which in shape and size greatly resembles a sandpiper, but on the water sits and swims like a duck, with its semi-webbed feet. This pretty bird is peculiarly fearless of mankind; and also deluded me on my first introduction into the idea that it was wounded. I was fishing in the Add, and saw my little friend swimming about in some shallow water left by the flood in a green meadow adjoining. I waded after it, and tried to catch it: several times nearly touching it with the landing-net before it fluttered away a few yards. At last, however, when it had had enough of the game, it gave perfect proof of its being quite uninjured by flying clean out of sight over the high hill of Dunadd and disappearing. Since then I have often got quite close to them and watched them for a long time, and I am glad to say I have never abused their confidence by taking their lives.

One specimen of a very rare bird, the brown or red-breasted snipe (*Macroramphus griseus*), was shot by my nephew, Harold Malcolm, in 1891. This bird is recorded twice over in Harvie Brown's "Fauna of Argyll and the Inner Hebrides," as the second and third specimen procured in Scotland. I note for the benefit of that very accurate observer, in case he should publish another edition of his book, that the bird "shot near Crinan, and exhibited by Dr. Edward Hamilton at a meeting of the Zoological Society," was the same bird "shot at Poltalloch by a son of Colonel Malcolm, on the 2nd of September 1891."

Two instances of curious "freaks" must conclude this prefatory chapter. A pure white woodcock was shot at Poltalloch, but the keeper who shot it and had it stuffed was allowed to take it away. I have always regretted that so rare and beautiful a specimen of albinism did not find its proper place in the interesting case in the hall of the Natural History Museum. The other was a rook, with the upper mandible of its beak prolonged to a length of some three inches, and curved and shaped like that of a curlew. The curious may see this singular malformation in the index case to the left of the central gallery, in company with the head of an equally remarkable pheasant presented by Lord Walsingham. It would have seemed almost impossible for any rook to feed with such a protuberance, but the bird had been observed for nearly three years, and was in quite good condition when killed.

The various sketches which follow were written at different times, many years apart, and describe typical days at different Highland sports on the West Coast. I leave them to speak for themselves, vouching for the accuracy of every fact recorded as having come under my personal observation.

CHAPTER II

FALLOW-DEER AT HOME

IT is a fine warm morning in the early part of September, and, after a pleasant walk across the hill, I have just come in sight of the sea, a narrow part of Loch Craignish lying immediately below me, at a distance of not more than four or five hundred yards. A large fir plantation, sloping down to the shore, clothes the hillside below me; there is a crisp, fresh feeling in the air, and the whole view is clear as only an Argyleshire landscape can be. These cliffs of Mull to the west, which look so distinct as they come down sheer to the blue water, are more than twenty miles distant; and Scarba, upon which one would expect to be able to "spy" the red deer with a good glass, is eight at least, as the crow flies. Below, the loch itself is studded with innumerable islands, varying in size from the small rocks which are barely visible at high tide, to Righ and Macaskan, which, between them, must attain a length of two miles. To the south-west, across the dreaded whirlpool of "Corrievreken,"[1] a faint

---

[1] I adopt Scott's spelling of the name. It is as well to say that my spelling of Gaelic names is in all cases phonetic. The true

outline of land is distinctly visible, and nearly due south the double peak of Jura stands out distinct and clear in the distance.

But what am I doing on the hillside? for I have not come here simply like Dr. Syntax, "in search of the picturesque." My express rifle is beside me, and I have also a coat, for I know that I shall probably spend the best part of the day on the hillside, and it is not impossible that there may be some showers before long, notwithstanding the almost supernatural brilliancy of sea and sky. However, I am prepared for any fate. I have my lunch, I have my flask, I have my coat, and I have my rifle and stalking-glass; and long experience has convinced me that I am in just the place to spend a happy day. I know that there are wild fallow-deer either in the large fir plantation below me, the hazel copses and bracken beds which clothe the brae-faces around me, or the natural cover on the face of Benan to the south; and I am sure that the hounds will find some of them, and hunt them round in my direction before the day is over. Whether I shall see anything more than does and fawns and small bucks not "worth a shot," or whether, if I do see a "muckle beast," he will come within

---

spelling contains a liberal allowance of b's and ch's not found in the ordinary guide-books or atlases, which take a line of their own, *e.g.* Black's Guide spells the above word "Corrivrekin." The *Times* Atlas reads "Corryvrekan."

shot of me ; or, again, whether I shall hit him if he does, are all questions of a more doubtful character. But I hope for the best, and, at any rate, I am determined to enjoy myself whatever happens. I have plenty of time before me, for the keepers have gone round to place the other rifles, and will then begin to hunt at the end of the wood more than a mile off, and I know that I can look about me without the least danger of anything passing me unperceived. Practice has sharpened my eyes and ears, and, even if a beast slips away without the hounds giving tongue, I shall be pretty sure to hear a stick snap, or the bracken rustle, and to see him before he is within shot of me.

I take out my glass and adjust it to focus, and first I turn it upon a small group of rocks close to the shore of the island opposite. Are there any seals on them? Ten years ago I counted twenty at a time basking and enjoying themselves there on such a day as this at low tide. Three— no, four, weird-looking cormorants, with their wings outstretched. No wonder Milton depicted Satan on the tree of knowledge in that form : it can hardly be called disguise. Then some herons, and, —yes, three long shapes, which an unpractised eye would take for rocks protruding above the tangle, but which I should know for seals, even without the occasional lazy motion of a tail or flapper, by which, I suppose, they are trying to get into a more comfortable position, just as Watts's sluggard "turns his sides and his shoulders and his heavy head" for the same purpose. Poor, pretty, persecuted beasts, I know you are mischievous, for I have seen you with salmon in your mouths, and poaching at the stake-nets; but an angler should not be too hard on you for that last fault, considering the way you tear them. How is it that, although I am always vowing that I never will shoot at you again,[1] I never can resist if I get an opportunity. It is not for your blubber, for I leave that to the boatmen; and it is not for your skin, for I have two, and should not know what to do with any more. I hope it is because of the well-founded confidence I feel in the probability of your escape, unless I get a chance at you on the rocks, stalking you from that very island opposite by creeping down the burn. It is surprising to think how many seals I have seen shot at in the water by good rifle-shots, and how few I have seen one penny the worse.

However, I am not after seals now, and I can watch those at my leisure with no bloodthirsty designs, and I look up and down the loch to see whether there are any more dog-like heads in view; for there is scarcely a ripple anywhere, as what wind there is, is from the west. I turn my glass on different distant objects in the water, to disclose in succession a flock of mergansers

[1] I never shoot at seals now. This was written a long time ago.

diving and swimming merrily along, many gulls of various species, some quaint little guillemots, some more cormorants fishing, and, lastly, an eider-duck with two young ones. I see the boat, too, which has come round from Duntroon; but the boatmen cannot have understood the message sent them in the morning, as they have gone into the landing-place instead of lying out half-way across, in case the deer take the water.

Some time has now elapsed since the keepers and hounds passed through the field below the plantation on the way to their starting-point, and I expect I shall soon hear the hounds. The pack is at rather a low ebb just now; but although they would be looked askance at in the Quorn Country, no doubt they will manage to "put some of them out of that," as the old keeper says. There are three foxhounds and three harriers, a small Poltalloch terrier, who will hunt anything, from a red-deer to a rat, and who is very useful in the high bracken beds, and a brown retriever. The gillies, also, will walk through the wood, and some of the best hounds will be kept coupled until a right beast is found.

There is something crossing the clear place in the wood where so many trees were blown down by the Tay Bridge gale: one, two, three, four—all does and fawns. I hope the hounds have not got upon them, for I hear the cry beginning, and they are certainly hunting something; no, it is all right, for I hear Woodman and Rachel on this side of where those deer passed, and they are coming this way. I take up my rifle and unbolt the hammer, and my heart beats a trifle quicker, for if the deer does take this line it will not be many minutes before he is here. There he is by the dyke, about 400 yards off, standing and thinking which way he will go next. The dyke is a rough stone wall, at least five feet in height; but if he means to make across the hill to Large, or to skirt the outside of the wood for the face of Benan, I shall be sure to get a shot at him. For fully a minute he stands hesitating; and I can see by his long brow antlers, and spreading, but not widely palmated horns, that he is a rare old stager, far superior in weight to the graceful creatures which ornament our English parks. Will he come? Alas! it is not to be; a turn and a bound, and he is off through the brackens and out of my sight; and I have the mortification of first seeing four of the hounds upon his track, and then hearing them pass below at a distance at which I might almost have shot the deer if it had been possible to see him in the thick cover.

My chance is gone for the present, but there is one rifle at the end between the two woods, and another in the "park" (*Anglicè*, field) below to the south, and one or other of them will surely get a shot. The first is out of my sight; but I know where the second should be, and mechanically I turn my glass upon the spot. Oh, shame! is that the way a soldier (and a colonel to boot) watches his pass? He is lying at full length in the heather, he has taken off his Norfolk jacket, and his white shirt shines conspicuous to the naked eye—worse, he has covered his head with a towel he brought with a view to bathing, and he is waving a bunch of brackens, and doubtless objurgating the flies and midges, while his rifle lies unheeded beside him. Well, no doubt, the insects are pretty bad down there out of the wind, but surely he will hear the hounds coming towards him, and rouse himself to a sense of his position. If not, I am well assured that no self-respecting deer will come within a quarter of a mile of such a conspicuous object. As I expected, the deer has turned, for I hear the cry of the hounds coming nearer to me, although still a long way off.

Is that a seal just off the small promontory a little this side of the landing-place? No, it is the deer, and he is making straight for the island opposite, looking neither to the right hand nor to the left. He swims very deep in the water, nothing but his head showing, with his horns well thrown back so as almost to touch his back, bringing his grand brow antlers prominently forward. Now, had the boatmen understood orders, he would have been ours, but in spite of my shouts and waving handkerchief, he is three parts of the way across before the boat is after him; the men pulling with a will to make up for lost time and neglected opportunities. He hears the splash of the oars and quickens his pace; and it is well for him that he does so, for the bow of the boat is actually touching his back before he reaches the shore. For a moment he stands and shakes himself, and then, trotting leisurely up the hill, is lost to sight in a bank of hazel. No doubt he thinks himself safe, but he is mistaken. All depends upon circumstances. If I can find the men, and they can catch some of the hounds, while there is time to go across after him, we may have him yet; for the island, although long, is narrow, and there is not much wood in it. He will, no doubt, be lying close, and, when found, will readily take to the water again to return to his home; but this time, at least, he will have no chance of escape in that quarter, for the boatmen will be on the alert and watching for him.

The baffled hounds, after fruitlessly baying for a minute or two on the shore, have straggled back into the cover. I despatch my lunch, and watch the herons lazily flying over the island opposite, counting over thirty, some of which, no doubt, are young ones of this year, bred upon the spot. Presently twelve black objects are seen crossing the field below in line, which I can recognise with the naked eye for a flock of the wild

American turkeys which have been introduced into the locality and thriven fairly well. Fine handsome fellows they are, with their glossy metallic plumage, and cinnamon wings and tail, but disappointing from a sporting point of view. It is almost impossible to persuade them to fly; but when they do, they look grand, swooping over your head from some woody bank above you, with hardly a motion of their great wings. It is, however, rather amusing sometimes to stalk them and shoot them, with a pea rifle, through the head or neck; to hit them anywhere else would be too easy for sport, besides spoiling the meat. Once fairly alarmed they seem to have discovered the secret of perpetual motion, and it is no easy matter to get a second tolerably easy shot. Their principal merits are that they are excellent birds for the table, and a great addition to the landscape.

This time I do not watch them for long, for I can study them at leisure at home from the window of my room. Never were there birds of more regular habits. The city clerk watching for his daily omnibus does not appear on the same place at the same time with more certainty. Unless something startling has happened to alarm them, you might safely set your watch by their movements, as they stroll along in line, morning and evening, picking the grass seeds as they go, with a rapid motion of head and neck which I have timed to take place a little more than a hundred times a minute. Next, a red object appears in the wood below me, and I seize my rifle as I recognise a roe well within shot. It raises its head to listen, and I cover it with the sight, but do not pull the trigger, for the motion has shown me that it has no horns; and, except in some very young plantation where the trees are being destroyed, I never shoot a doe.

The hounds are hunting again in wood below me, and a shout or two shows that the beaters are approaching, when I see another deer in the water just where the first one crossed. This time the boat is on the lookout, and from my watch-tower I see him caught and bound before he has got half-way across. He is, however, a reluctant and recalcitrant captive; for when he has been hauled in on one side of the boat, he jumps out once upon the other before he is fairly secured. He looks a pretty good beast, lighter in colour than the other, but certainly not so large. To-day it seems that the boatmen are to have all the sport, which surprises me, as the deer have not been shot at or particularly hard pressed by the hounds. I suppose it is the fine day and the unrippled sea which makes them so ready for a bath. However, it is a good opportunity to signal to the boatmen; the gillies are near, and the hounds will be easily caught, and we can see what we can do with the big beast on the island before we determine the fate of our unfortunate captive. One man is sent round to fetch the other rifles and bring them down to the shore, while I and the keeper make for the same point through the wood, and before we reach the boat we have caught Prudence and Woodman, who will be quite enough to find and start the buck that got away from us this morning. As we announce our intention of sailing or rowing home, which may make us rather late, one of the party prefers to walk back across the hill; so we start off with six men in all—two keepers, the boatmen, and ourselves, with two hounds and the brown retriever, whose presence is not at all relished by the fallow-buck which lies at the bottom of the boat, with his legs tied together and his horns tied to the seat in a workman-like manner. We examine him, and pronounce him to be five years old and very fat; the palm of the horn is widening, but the brow antlers are still short, and, as he has two years of growth before him, I make up my mind that whatever may happen to his companion, when the council is held to determine his fate, my voice shall be given in favour of mercy.

A very few minutes bring us to the island, and we take up our positions. I mount guard on a knoll near the landing-place, from which I can see the whole breadth of the island except the wooded banks, which slope down to the shore on either side, while my companion takes his place farther to the south, where he is almost certain to get a shot, if, as is probable, the buck has not left the cover which was his point in the morning. A few old black-cocks, glossy enough, although not in the full perfection of their winter plumage, rise and fly lazily across to the mainland on either side, and there is a fresh breadth of sea to explore with the glass, more ruffled, because more exposed to the now stiffening breeze. The mainland on the west is some distance off; and the nearest island on the same side, a rocky precipice with hardly grazing enough upon it for a goat, must be nearly a mile away. However, I have not long to spend in contemplation, for, before the hounds have begun to give tongue, I recognise something brushing a path through the long brackens below me, and a smart run brings me within shot of the beast, galloping away as hard as he can about 150 yards off, end on towards me. Another moment and he will be out of sight. Shall I shoot? At least I determine not to repeat a feat accomplished some years before, when I planted an expanding ball well between the haunches of a deer in a similar position with deadly effect, actually cutting off its tail, which my companions proposed to present to me as a testimonial, with a suitable inscription. Head or nothing, here goes! and the ball whistles between his horns just before he passes out of sight below the brae. My companion has seen him, and fired a fruitless and melancholy shot at him at a long range; but never mind, he will have to come back again, and, once I make out his intentions, I know the island sufficiently well to cut him off whatever point he makes for. Vain hope! to my great surprise I see him in the water again on the west side of the island. I join my companion and we watch him with our glasses. Surely an unwounded beast would not have taken the water at a wholly unknown point without a notion where to make for. It does not, however, take long to convince us, from the pace he is swimming, that he is quite unhurt. It is too late to get the boat, although he must be in the water a long time. As the biggest fish are those that get off the hook, so the length of those brow antlers and the span of those horns gradually increase as we watch him ploughing his way across the bay. Once or twice we think, or try to think, that he means to turn, in which case he is ours; but the hope is vain, and at last we see him land and trot up the island in the distance, unscathed and safe; for, even if there were time, we have no right to pursue him there. Slowly we collect our forces, and join in lamentations over the deer departed—not alas! the "dear deceased," to quote Hood's wonderful pun from the "Epping Hunt." Next we land, and liberate our captive, after marking his ear in order that we may recognise and calculate his growth on some future occasion, and then up with the sail. Two beats take us out of Loch Craignish, and as we watch the setting sun purpling the rocks over Jura, and lazily discuss the pipe of peace, we think of the lines so inimitably illustrated by Caldecott :—

"So they hunted and they hollo'd till the setting of the sun,
   An' they'd nought to bring away at last, when th' hunting-
     day was done.
   Then one unto the other said, 'This huntin' doesn't pay,
   But we'n powler't up an' down a bit an' had a rattlin' day.
                Look ye there!'"

It must not be supposed that all our expeditions are as unsuccessful as the one I have just described. I chose it for description partly because it is an almost literal and exact account of what occurred on the last occasion I was out after the deer, and partly because I thought there was some spark of originality in describing a failure. Many deer are doubtless missed upon the hillside, but few indeed in the smoking-room or in the pages of sporting chronicles. There was one occasion, ever to be marked with white, when, as I occupied the same position, two grand beasts trotted out of the hazel bank between me and the dyke, about sixty yards off, before I had been in my place half-an-hour. I chose the one which had the finest head, and shot him through the neck, and, hastily putting a fresh cartridge into my single-barrelled Henry, fired a snapshot at the second, without success, as he galloped off. By the time that I had loaded again he had stopped for a moment at the dyke, either to wait for his "neighbour" or to look before he leaped. It was a long distance, but then he was standing broadside to me, and, putting up the 200 yards' sight, and taking it full I fired again. A sudden start, a turn, and he disappeared into the hazel bank behind him. I ran hurriedly on to the end of it to see where he went, but I might have spared myself the trouble, for when the keepers and hounds came up he was lying dead not twenty yards from where I shot at him with a ball through his heart. A noble beast, the largest I had killed or seen killed up to that date. He weighed one hundred and ninety-two pounds clean; his companion a hundred and sixty-seven. The weight of the deer first killed, which had the better head, was by no means unusual or remarkable; for these wild fallow-deer have what they like best, a wide range and abundance and variety of food, which makes them on an average far heavier than their domestic cousins, and a full-grown buck is seldom less than one hundred and fifty pounds.[1] For the benefit of any one who may wish to institute a comparison, I should say that the weights of the deer are given

---

[1] My record of 192 lbs. has been twice beaten, since I killed one of 202 lbs. in 1891, and another of the great weight of 204 lbs. fell to Lord Malcolm's rifle in 1897.

as they are brought in off the hill, with the head and the horns still on, but "gralloched" and bled. Their horns are not nearly so broad and shovel-like as those of a park buck; some run to points almost like a red deer's. I have heard various suggested explanations of this, but none satisfactory to my mind, so I content myself with merely stating the fact. To conclude the catalogue of their qualities, their venison is the finest known.

Fallow-deer are naturally frequenters of woods, only leaving the cover to feed in the early gloaming, and in the evening just before the twilight, and, therefore, cannot be stalked in the proper sense of the word. I have, however, often succeeded in getting a shot walking quietly through the covers in the evenings, and keeping a sharp lookout in the open places. Even when startled at your approach, the deer generally stand for a moment, and give an opportunity for a snapshot. In the smaller woods it is as well, in the first instance at any rate, to try to start them by simply sending two or three beaters through, as they do not travel so far or so fast as when the hounds are after them. I have never known an unwounded fallow-deer actually run down by the hounds, although they might, no doubt, be occasionally caught by a more numerous and swifter pack. The best sort of hound for the purpose is one with a good nose and solid of bone and sinew, and, above all, plenty of tongue to tell the soporific sportsman of the approach of the deer. I remember one distinguished literary character (now a judge of the High Court) who insisted on taking Homer out with him on one of our expeditions, and, although he loudly protests to this day that he kept a good lookout all the time, and that nothing came anywhere near him, he will never persuade the keeper or myself that the deer did not pass within a hundred yards of him. Horace is our authority for the statement that Homer was not above taking an occasional nap himself; and I can well believe that, on that fine autumn day, on the pleasant hillside, he was the cause of sleep in another.

Although on most occasions the position of the rifles is changed more than once, there is no doubt that many sportsmen look upon such a deer hunt or drive as monotonous and dull, and only take part in one, quite unnecessarily, out of good nature. It must be admitted, too, that on a still, muggy day, in a sheltered place, the midges can make themselves extremely disagreeable. It is curious how much more they attack some people than others, and with what different effect. For myself, to quote the expressive sentence of an Irish milkmaid, "It is not the bit they ate of me that I grudge; it's just the everlasting trampling they kape up." Not a sign of their attacks remains upon me in the evening, whereas I have seen the face of one of their victims covered with good-sized bumps which did not disappear for more than a week.

After all, it is a good deal a question of temperament whether the sport ought really to be called monotonous. To me, "custom cannot stale its infinite variety." I have described a day in a particular place—certainly, to my eyes, one of the loveliest spots in Scotland—but there is no place which has not its objects of interest for eyes that are open to see them. In one single August morning I have seen no less than eight woodcocks flushed, each carrying a young one curiously huddled up between its beak and feet; and, on another occasion, one ran up within a yard of me, snapping its bill and making a curious hissing noise when I picked up its half-grown baby, which, it is needless to say, I had no intention of hurting. But the commonest birds and beasts have an interest, as you watch them, unconscious of your presence. The startled surprise of the hare, rabbit, or squirrel, which, after feeding for some time quite close to you, suddenly discovers that you are really alive, has its comical element. Then thousands of lovely mosses, and ferns of all kinds, from the tall Osmunda to the tiny film fern, more like a moss (if one may say so without a bull) than some of the true mosses, disclose themselves unsought in places where, as yet, they are safe from the predatory instincts of collectors. The true botanist or tourist does little harm; but a new race has sprung up, of whom it is difficult to speak or think with patience, who have discovered the commercial value of ferns, and are rapidly destroying what is rare and beautiful. I know one exquisite Highland loch, of which the most remarkable and beautiful feature was the Osmunda, which fringed its banks in veritable bushes. Last year, an enterprising collector fairly stripped the accessible portions of the banks, and carried away three cart-loads of roots! I do not know if he could swim, but I should have been very glad to have given him the opportunity of learning to do so in his clothes.

The same hounds which hunt the fallow-deer also serve for following the roe; and indeed, if they had the choice, would probably select the latter amusement (as the scent is stronger or more attractive). The roe prefer the natural birch-woods and young plantations to the high woods and thick bracken, and trust more to their cunning than their speed to elude pursuit. Their endless turns and devices, and the fact that they usually run in a ring, and never go far in front of the hounds, make a roe hunt very amusing to watch, particularly as in the open cover on a hillside one can often see the whole course of the hunt for an hour together. I have seen an old buck, with the hounds after it, push a doe out of its couch in the bracken, and take its place, thus providing a substitute in a manner which did more credit to its ingenuity than to its gallantry. The hounds frequently run them down, wearying them out much as a stoat does a rabbit, by perseverance rather than speed.

I may conclude with the story of a roe hunt in another place, for which I cannot vouch my personal knowledge. Some years ago the roe had increased to a mischievous extent in a young plantation, and the fiat was issued for a massacre on a large scale. All who were willing to assist were invited, and a mixed crowd of farmers, shepherds, and keepers made their appearance, each with a gun or rifle over his shoulder, and a flask of whisky in his pocket. Boys, gillies, hounds, and collies were employed in starting the game and keeping it on foot; and from an early hour a terrific bombardment continued—slugs, buck-shot, and bullets flying in all directions. The head-keeper, to give his own account, soon retired into a dry ditch and prayed, thus providing, as far as he could, for his bodily safety and spiritual welfare. Happily no one was killed or even wounded. The next morning one of the farmers came and asked him, with an air of mystery, if he had paid his boys. He replied in the affirmative. "And did they all come for their money?" "Yes," he said. "Then," said the questioner with an air of relief, "it will be a roe that you will find lying under the dyke a wee bit west of the withered ash tree."

CHAPTER III

CHASING THE ROE

"I watched a roe," says St. John, in a well-known passage of his "Wild Sports of the Highlands," "stripping the leaves off a long bramble shoot. My rifle was aimed at his heart, and my finger was on the trigger, but I made some excuse or other to myself for not killing him, and left him undisturbed. His beauty saved him." I am afraid that with most sportsmen on the war-path the sporting aspect is apt to prevail over the æsthetic, and they do not often show the same forbearance as the genial author of the brightest of sporting records; but if beauty could prevail to soften the heart, no animal would be more likely to reach old age than a roebuck.

What a beautiful thoroughbred-looking creature he is—a very fairy of the woods! A roe, threading his path through birch and bracken, or standing for a moment in some open glade with graceful head turned towards the intruder, looks, what he is, no trespasser, but tenant in fee by right of birth and prescription as one of the oldest inhabitants. His big brother the stag is

The haunt of the Roe.

perhaps a grander object, but, as far as grace of motion is concerned, clumsy in comparison. His dappled cousin the fallow-buck may have come over before the Conqueror, but is undoubtedly a foreign intruder of Asiatic origin, although he has been sufficiently long settled in his adopted home to acquire all the rights and privileges of an English citizen, including the doubtful advantage of having paid toll to Robin Hood and his merry men in Sherwood Forest, and tithe to the Church in the person of Friar Tuck. Still these country cousins must be content with a respectful recognition of their charms, quite different from the hearty admiration which any true John Bull or Sandy bestows upon his indigenous kinsman. They shared the society and provided the food and clothing of our palæolithic ancestors, and their bones and horns are found in cave and tumulus with those of hyæna and bear, along with the flint arrowheads and knives which killed and skinned them. And if the claim of ancient lineage and descent is not acknowledged in this revolutionary age, the roe can appeal to the sympathies of the most ardent democrat on the ground of his unquenchable love of liberty. Stag and hind, fallow buck and doe, take kindly enough to a semi-domestic life, and are familiar objects in parks and paddocks all over England; but the roe does not readily brook confinement within a narrow fence, running round and round, seeking an outlet for escape, until death terminates his captivity. I believe there are still a few roe in some very large parks, such as Windsor and Petworth; but in the former of these, at any rate, it is probable that the roe existed long before it was enclosed, and such apparent exceptions only prove the rule.

Although they do not appreciate confinement in a paddock, it is easy to tame a fawn, and it makes a delightful pet until it attains to years of indiscretion. A tame roe used to follow the children everywhere round the old castle of Duntroon, and even up the stairs and into the rooms. One of his little playfellows had been obliged to give up his room to a gentleman who had come to stay there, and the surprise of the guest was unbounded when the head and neck of a roe protruded through his half-open door. "Dear me!" he said; "game must be extremely plentiful in these parts!"

Yet just as a kitten would be the most delightful of pets except for its unfortunate habit of growing into a cat, so a roe, and especially a buck, becomes too much of a handful as a pet when it grows up. Their beautiful little horns are both sharp and dangerous, and a tame roebuck very nearly put an old woman off the road and into the Crinan Canal by its obtrusive attentions. It meant no harm: it really expected to get a lump of the rock-salt with which it had usually been rewarded for its caresses; but the old dame did not appreciate its uncanny approaches, and narrowly escaped with her life.

Opinions differ as to the merits of the roe from the point of view of the sportsman, but this, I think, is mainly owing to the fact that so many are killed in the course of the winter battues. No doubt they add an element of the picturesque to the bag as they are arranged in line before the door of the lodge, with blackgame, woodcocks, pheasants, hares, and rabbits, and perhaps a few odd capercailzie; but I for one would always prefer not to pull the trigger of a shot-gun at an object like a calf, although I have had many an interesting and exciting day after them with the rifle. It is true that "old masters" like Colquhoun and St. John agree in recommending shot as preferable to ball for roe-shooting, on the ground that fewer are wounded; but those who humanely take the advice of these writers do not sufficiently appreciate the great advance which has been made since their time in the manufacture of weapons of precision, of improved range, velocity, and accuracy, combined with lower elevation. I do not profess to be a first-rate shot with a rifle, but I do not remember losing a single wounded buck, although I have accounted for a very large number during the last twenty-five years. The hounds, if you have them with you, or even retrievers or spaniels, soon come up to a roe with a bullet in his body; but, although a charge of No. 5 shot aimed well forward will roll one over like a rabbit, young sportsmen are apt to get excited when the beaters shout "Deer forward!" and many shots are fired when, owing to the thickness of the cover or the distance of the object, there is no reasonable chance of securing the quarry. I believe that many carry away a few pellets under such circumstances, and that if the roe could be consulted in the matter they would unhesitatingly express their preference for the bullet.

Perhaps the most amusing way of shooting roe, when the ground is suitable, is for the guns to take up positions on heights commanding fairly open glades in the woods, where the cover can be drawn by hounds. The scent is very strong, and almost any kind of dogs take to it kindly, but a scratch pack of otter-hounds, or old or slow fox-hounds, are the best for the purpose. A really fast pack would drive the roe too quick and too far. The object should be to get together a few steady hounds with plenty of "tongue," resolute on the scent, with perhaps some bustling terriers to start the buck out of the thickets and bracken. Unless too much pressed, roe are inclined to trust more to cunning than to speed, while their habit of running in a circle and their disinclination to break cover give the sportsmen every chance. But perhaps my readers will be best able to judge of the nature of the sport if I describe one of the many occasions when not merely my heart, but my body as well, has been " in the Highlands a-chasing the deer."

It is a splendid September morning in the much-slandered climate of Argyleshire, clear shining after rain, and the waggonette with its load of sportsmen bowls cheerily along the straight level road across the Crinan Moss in the direction of the Canal. On the right, Jura, Scarba, and the high hills of Mull show themselves across the bay. The tide is low as we cross the bridge over the Add, a small fleet of mergansers are making their way up stream, the exposed sandbanks are crowded with gulls and plovers, while two or three solemn-looking herons, knee-deep in water, are enjoying "the contemplative birds' recreation." A short turn to the left along the road between the Crinan Canal and the beautiful wooded and fern-clad brae brings us to Dunardry Lock, the place where the keepers are waiting for us, and where the *Linnet* has just arrived with her cargo of passengers from the north. The usual miscellaneous-looking collection of tourists are disporting themselves on the bank, while some are offering a feeble resistance to a small band of infant marauders who are pestering them to purchase milk, fern roots, bunches of heather, and "sweeties," or frankly demanding blackmail without any offer of an equivalent; others, with legitimate curiosity, are inspecting the queer-looking scratch lot that are straining at their couples on the bridge. Well may they wonder what the pack is intended to pursue, composed as it is of four foxhounds, a draft from the York and Ainstey, two light-coloured wire-haired terriers of our own particular breed, a small Sussex spaniel, and York, an ancient black retriever, stone deaf, and grey about the muzzle, but good for a year or two of work still. The party descend from the "machine" and equip and arm themselves with waterproofs, rifles, flasks, and lunch. Barnakil, the wood we mean to hunt to-day, is one of those old natural birch woods which are becoming yearly rarer, in consequence of the ravages of the sheep; but which formerly clothed half the brae faces in Argyleshire. The leader of the party leaves us to take up a position where a small hillock covered with old Scotch firs overlooks a queer boggy flat surrounded by covert on all sides, and intersected with open drains and burns; and as he takes his seat among a heap of boulders, I can see how well his grey suit harmonises with its surroundings. He measures nearly six feet and a half in his stockings, but his by no means scant proportions are almost invisible before I have got very far from him. The next to leave me is one who has watched for the roe on these hills long

CHASING THE ROE

before I did, knows every pass in the wood, and can conjecture the probable course of a hunted buck almost infallibly. A truer sportsman never existed—alas! that I should have to use the past tense. In the hunting-field, by the salmon river, in the grouse butts, or at a hot corner, equally trustworthy; best known, perhaps, in his later years on the racecourse, where he loved to see Queen's Birthday, Nunthorpe, and other horses bred by himself, carry his colours to victory, although he seldom made a bet. He takes up his position on the brae face to the right, while I hurry on to my pass, which I reach about noon. We did not make a very early start, nor was it necessary to do so; four or five hours' hunting is quite enough to exhaust the capacities of a limited pack. The heathery ridge where I take my place stands high in the centre of the wood, overlooking on all sides little valleys, or rather glades, through which the roe are likely to pass; but, although I can see well from my point of vantage, it will be necessary to keep a sharp lookout, as the colour of a roe's hide bears a strong protective resemblance to the tint of the bracken, now rapidly turning brown, and there is more or less covert everywhere around me of which the light-footed beasts will be sure to take every advantage. They will not draw attention to their presence when hunted, as do the blundering fallow-deer, but flit noiselessly past like ghosts of that variety which does not indulge in blood-curdling groans and clanking of chains; but quiet as they may be, I can hear something already—the deep notes of Wayward and Valorous; and I instinctively clutch my rifle as they seem at first to be coming in my direction. I catch just a glimpse of a tawny skin crossing the hill about a quarter of a mile behind me, and then of the two hounds; but soon they seem to have changed their direction, and a loud report, followed by an ominous silence, tells me that I am not likely to see that roe alive, and that I have a little leisure to look about me. To the west, across the flat peat moss, I can see the mouth of the Add spanned by the bridge we recently crossed, with the low part of Jura just visible behind. In the far north the double peak of Ben Cruachan is just visible as a pale shadow above another range of hills. The wild blue rock-pigeons are flying to and fro along the slaty cairn which bounds the glade immediately below me, while, overhead, cormorant, gull, and heron are winging a stately and steady flight between Lochs Fyne and Crinan. But already the hounds are giving tongue again, and I must attend to business.

About three hundred yards away some sheep take a short scamper, then gather in a cluster, and stare in their silly way in the direction from which the hounds are coming. No doubt the roe is there, but he is keeping under the height; for I fail to catch a sight of him until, a few minutes later, he suddenly appears daintily tripping towards me along the very ridge on which I am seated in ambush, and stopping now and again to listen. He is not more than two hundred yards away, and I can see that he is a buck, and a good one too. He stands for a moment uncertain what course to pursue; there certainly is danger behind him, but he also seems to have a sort of instinctive knowledge of something not altogether right in front. I get a good look at him with my field-glasses, and admire the beautiful little head, which has its full complement of six points. Unless he turns, those graceful horns ought to be mine, for he can hardly fail to pass within sixty yards of me, and although he is not a very large mark I am comfortably seated, and have not the breathless stalker's excuse for a wide shot, nor the novice's stumbling-block of excitement. Another minute and he is started at the renewed music of the hounds, and is passing at a swift but easy trot broadside below me. St. Hubert direct my aim! I pull the trigger, and the ball of the express strikes him a little far back, but fortunately not enough so to damage his haunch, and he sinks to rise no more.

Leaving my rifle, I scramble down the stones through the brushwood, and have just time to administer the *coup de grâce* before the dogs arrive, and to chide them back in the direction of the keepers before they can tear the flesh of the dead roe. It is not always prudent to leave one's rifle behind. On a former occasion I was not so fortunate. A roebuck had crossed me at the very pass I now occupy, not twenty yards off, and I rolled him over and over; but when I had almost got up to him, he jumped up and bolted off as if nothing had happened, and "I was left lamenting." No doubt the ball had either struck his horn or just grazed the spine, merely stunning him for a moment, for I could detect no trace of a wound upon him with my glass as he galloped away, and he got clear off, though the hounds were close upon his trail.

By the time I have done justice to the excellent lunch, consisting of half a cold grouse, a buttered roll, and a slice of cake, washed down with a little whisky and water, at least two more roe have passed me within range; in one case age, and in the other sex, protected them. In neither instance were they being hunted, but they had evidently been disturbed either by the dogs or the keepers, and were trying to steal away. How easily that little buck with mere buttons of horns negotiates the stone dyke below, with the wire on the top of it! The doe knows her way about better, and does not take the trouble to jump the fence, but makes straight for the little passage through the dyke, which arches over a small stream hardly big enough to be dignified with the title of burn. I am half through a meditative pipe before the flight of three or four black-game and a late woodcock heralds the approach of the keepers with terriers, retriever, and two of the hounds coupled up. They report progress: another buck has been killed, and the other two hounds are away after a big one which has taken right across the moss to Ballimore. Probably they will have lost him when he crossed the river, and will be coming back by this time. Donald is off after them with orders to meet them at the far end of the wood near Dunadd, and they are going round there to hunt the covert back this way. They will not let the remaining hounds go unless a fair buck is started, as we are short-handed as it is, and cannot afford to lose any more time after does and small trash.

So the day passes with varied incident, and when we make our way to the road at about half-past four, we have got altogether four bucks and a good yeld doe, the latter of which fell to the shot-gun of the youngest of the party, who had been stationed near the edge of a young plantation of firs, with orders to kill anything he could, as they were "doing mischief" there. A good bag, but nothing to compare with those of thirty years ago, when the roe literally swarmed in all the natural woods round the canal. Then, however, they were greatly encouraged and preserved for the benefit of the lady of Poltalloch, who was a most deadly shot with a pea-rifle, and devoted to the sport of hunting the roe. Then also the pack was far more complete, and many legends are still handed down by oral tradition of the feats of Towler, the old otter-hound, who never left the scent, and, when he was bidden to a roe-hunt, frequently interpreted the invitation like Mr. Jorrocks—"where I dines I sleeps"—and returned in the morning after a day and night out, dissipated-looking, rotund, but contented.

There is a legend, for which I decline to vouch, that he once pursued a roe for three days, when the two were seen about twenty yards apart, looking as if neither could go an inch farther.

It is pleasant enough, too, to stroll through the woods of an evening, and look out for the roe in the open spaces. Many a good buck has fallen to my rifle in Kilchurn banks, Bar-na-slue, and Kilbride; but it is not so easy now to get quietly through the woods as it was before the succession of gales denuded whole hillsides of their plantations, twisting and knotting the great fir-trees like spillikins. Till then the paths were beautifully kept, but it has taken years to make them at all practicable, and for a long time they were in many places quite impassable. A rook rifle is good enough for a steady shot at this work. For a roe-hunt I prefer an express, as one may have to fire long shots at uncertain ranges, and often at a moving object; but, stealing through the woods and coming upon the deer at shorter distances and quite undisturbed, it is easy enough to put a small bullet in a fatal spot. Even if a buck is startled by seeing you before you catch sight of him, he is so curious that he is almost sure to stand to look round after running a few steps, sufficiently long to give you a good chance. Mr. Egremont Lascelles, who used to be particularly fond of a still stalk, and was most successful at the sport, told me a curious incident which occurred to him when after roe. He came upon a buck standing in an open space in one of the Poltalloch woods, and saw that it was looking at him. He advanced cautiously with his rifle cocked to see how near to it he could approach, and, to his unbounded surprise, it allowed him to walk right up to it, take it by the horn, and put the knife into its throat. Of course, he supposed that it had been wounded, or that there was something the matter with it, but it turned out to be in perfectly good condition, with all its organs healthy, and without a sign or symptom of so much as a scratch.

The wood immediately behind Poltalloch House has been long maintained as a complete sanctuary for roe, no shot being fired at them there. As a consequence, they have always been both numerous and tame there. It is hardly possible to pass through any of the short walks behind the garden without seeing one or more of these graceful creatures, and many a time have I taken aim at them as I returned from an afternoon after the rabbits in the cairn, but of course never drew trigger. They are not taken in by the apparent danger, as they are quite aware of the regulations of the establishment, and buck, doe, and fawn alike face the deadly tube with a confidence bred of the knowledge that in that wood it is quite innocuous. Long may they flourish there unharmed, giving infinite pleasure to all who delight in studying wild nature!

It is perhaps rather bathos to turn from their æsthetic and sporting qualities to gastronomic uses. I cannot say that I personally have a very high opinion of the flesh of roe as food. It differs in flavour from venison, mutton, or hare, although it has a smack of each and all. Dressed *à la Chasseur* with preserved cherries it is very good, and a haunch larded with a little mutton-fat is palatable; but my mind recoils with horror from Colquhoun's suggestion that bucks ought to be shot in the winter, when they have lost their horns, because they are then better eating. For my part, I would rather have one fine roe's head than a wilderness of haunches; and as my eye rests gratefully on some of my beautiful trophies, I do not envy the base epicurean who would sacrifice such lasting pleasure for the doubtful privilege of feasting on inferior mutton.

CHAPTER IV

FIRST IMPRESSIONS OF DEER-STALKING

THERE are some days and some events that can never be effaced from the memory. It is more than thirty years since that upon which I made my first futile attempt to shoot a stag; yet as I sit down to write every detail of the long day seems fresh and vivid, and the memory which so often fails to recall events of far greater importance for once is not at fault. Let the reader go back with me to the beautiful valley of the North Esk, and a September morning in the early seventies.

I was then staying at Millden with the first Lord Cairns. We had had good sport with the grouse; but there were no red deer upon the ground, and my excitement was great when an invitation arrived from Lord Dalhousie to join in a deer drive in the adjacent forest of Invermark. Two of us were to go, and Lord Cairns and the elder members of the party waived their claims in favour of myself and a young nephew of our host. The start was to be an early one, as the rendezvous was at the Castle, seven miles up the glen, and we were to be there not later than eight o'clock. We were up and dressed soon after six, and seven saw us under way driving up the narrow glen by the road which winds along the valley within sight of the beautiful river. The North Esk is always a picturesque object in the landscape, but on this occasion its aspect was peculiarly wild and grand. Twenty-four hours of violent and almost tropical rainfall had occasioned the heaviest flood that I ever witnessed during five years of visits to its neighbourhood, and it had risen more than ten feet, and swept away nearly every foot-bridge along its course; while stooks and haycocks, whirled along by the turbid torrent, told a melancholy tale of devastation and ruin. The rain was still falling as the dog-cart bore us towards our destination, but breaks in the sky promised better weather later in the day.

I suppose there are not many now who remember the Lord Dalhousie of that day, who received us at breakfast on our arrival, with old Horatio Ross, the father of my great friend, Edward, the first Queen's prizeman, sitting beside him. Old Dalhousie was crippled with gout, his fingers being swollen and almost distorted; but he could still make good practice at driven grouse at a short range with a little 20-bore gun and a light charge. He ruled the glen with a rod of iron, and asserted and exercised rights over his tenants and labourers, the mention of which would make the hair of the politician stand upright in these more democratic days. Needless to say he received us hospitably, but his first sentence was a sad damper to our enthusiasm. There could be no deer drive that day. The wind was wrong, and even if this obstacle had not been insurmountable, the swollen condition of the burns and rivers would have made it impossible to drive a large tract of country. Our disappointment and misery were apparent in our crestfallen faces; but dear old Ross soon reassured us. Of course, we should have a stalk, and let us take it from him that it would be far better fun than the drive we had missed. A faint, and perhaps not altogether sincere, protest against his giving up his sport was offered; but he would not hear of our not having a day in the forest after we had come so far; and nine o'clock saw us tramping off in charge of the stalker and a couple of gillies for the first corrie, about five miles from the Castle.

The ponies stood saddled at the door, but we were told that we must do without them. Later in the day perhaps, if the weather cleared, it would be possible for them to follow us to the scene of action; but for the present they would only be a hindrance, as it would be impossible for them to ford even what on ordinary days would have been dry watercourses or shallow rivulets. The difficulty as to two going together was solved by the usual process of tossing for first shot, and fortune favoured me. On we splashed over bog and moor, often having to make a long circuit before we could cross any running water, large packs of grouse rising many gunshots away as we advanced. It had been a wild night, and they all had their heads up and were ready to take alarm at the slightest danger. It was bitterly cold, and the rain had been sleet on the high hills; but we were warm enough with excitement and exercise; and welcomed the "brave north-easter" as if we had been Kingsley himself. An eagle soared over the highest peak in the distance, and before we got to the spying place a small flock of ptarmigan ran along close to our feet, and only took to flight upon compulsion and under protest. At another time such objects would have filled us with excited delight, but to-day we were after our first stag, and any meaner creature seemed hardly worthy of notice. It seemed as though we should never begin the real sport of the day, although we had certainly lost no time in covering the ground on our way out. At last Donald reached a large rock just below the summit of the brae, overlooking a corrie, bounded on the opposite side by a steep and rocky hillside. With what eagerness we watched his impassive face as he made himself comfortable, steadied his glass with his stick, and took the usual deliberate survey of all the ground around him! We also did our best to spy; but the work was new to us, and we did not know where to look, or we could hardly have failed to

Sonne obientables bonsts

find for ourselves the herd that was pointed out to us when our guide rose to his feet and shut up his glass with the unconcerned air which at that stage of the proceedings is part of the stock-in-trade of every stalker. There they were, nearly a hundred deer, as it seemed to me, scattered—too much scattered, alas!—over a green spot on the hillside opposite, not far from the summit level. There were some shootable beasts among them, and it would not be difficult to get within shot; but we must lose no time, as they were all standing up and moving about, very restless, after the storm. There was no need to press us—we were young and in good training—and we dashed along after our leader, copying his every movement in the most approved style, and rather sorry that we were allowed to remain erect, and could not ford a river or crawl through a bog to show our zeal for the sport. I cannot honestly describe any moving incidents of the stalk. I have since had a good many days in the forest, but I hardly ever remember an easier approach. The wind was right, and all we had to do was to make a long détour, climb the back of the steep peak opposite, and come over the summit level under cover, right upon the deer, which (as all know) are much easier to get at from above than from below, or on the level. It was a long walk and a stiff climb, but that was all, and we were soon looking down upon a forest of horns, breathless and excited, but hopeful. I shall never forget that sight: there were plenty of stags well within shot, and to my unpractised eye all of them were, of course, quite big enough to kill. But such was not Donald's opinion: there were just one or two worth a shot, and the one he selected as the right beast was nearly on the outside of the herd, at least a hundred and fifty yards off. My airy confidence was rather shaken, but I was a fair target shot and had done some execution among fallow-deer and roe with the rifle, and was quite ready and willing to fire at the mark offered. Again I was stopped. The herd was moving uphill and I must wait till the beast came a good deal nearer. Meantime I could watch it and keep my sight upon it if I liked until I was told to shoot. The loser of the toss also got his rifle ready, "in case I missed," and the period of suspense commenced.

I do not suppose we waited long, but it really seemed a century. The chilly wind whistled over the hill behind me, and I gradually got colder and colder, and my fingers more and more benumbed; while the restless quadrupeds walked about without my particular stag coming appreciably nearer, although some of his companions must have been within fifty yards. By the time that I was told to shoot, I do not believe that I could have hit a haystack, and, worst of all, my stag had got rather farther instead of nearer. But it was now or never, as he showed every sign of an intention of going round the corner of a knob out of sight. Alas for the toss and the lucky penny! If this was to be the first shot, I had far better have lost. However, bang went the rifle, off went the bullet — where Heaven knows — followed by a second from my companion's rifle, and away went the whole herd, more frightened than hurt.

Since then I have fired a good many shots at deer with fair success, but occasionally I have been guilty of misses which could only be described by the word disgraceful. It is a melancholy moment when a stag gallops off unscathed which you really ought to have made certain of with a bow and arrow; and the only thing to do is to bear the stalker's reproachful glances with resignation, and own up to your shortcomings like a man. Depend upon it, in the smoking-room in the evening you will be more pitied than condemned if you condescend to tell the absolute truth without excuse or evasion. "Did you ever see such a miss as that?" said a relative of my own—one of the finest shots that ever handled a rifle—to the stalker, after letting off a stag broadside under a hundred yards in a good position, on a clear day, with every condition in his favour. "Aye, I have, sir, mony a one," was the reply, and there was no more to be said. But on this occasion my disappointment was unmixed with any flavour of self-reproach. I did not expect to hit the beast, and indeed it would have been more or less of a fluke if I had. Moreover I solaced myself with the thought that, if I had been allowed to shoot earlier, when I had wished to do so, the result might have been different.

Here I pause for a moment to discuss the question whether the advice invariably given by experts to beginners to wait for a deer to rise is always sound. There can of course be no doubt that a deer lying down presents a much smaller mark than one standing up and feeding; but I question whether the delay, often tedious and protracted, does not more than counterbalance this advantage. Of course it is to some extent a question of temperament; a phlegmatic man may be able to contemplate a fine stag reposing at a short distance from his rifle for an hour or more with an absolute assurance of success; but, for myself, I always feel my confidence waning as time passes; and if the wait is a long one, I am very apt to disgrace myself when the critical moment arrives. I cannot, however, pose as an authority upon the subject. I have never rented a forest, although I have killed a fair number of stags in the course of my autumnal wanderings; and a rule so universally observed by the most skilful and practised sportsmen must be right in the main. Personally, however, I would rather take an indifferent chance than wait an indefinite time, feeling my courage oozing out of my finger-ends; and where there was no one to say me nay, I have sometimes taken my own course with success.

But to return to my first day at Invermark. I had missed my first chance, but all was not lost, and we started at once on a desperate attempt to cut off the herd, which was heading at a gallop for the neighbouring corrie. Down we ran, leaping over peat hags and scrambling across boulders, and my companion duly scored his miss at the herd, still moving at a fairly long range, with even better excuse for failure than myself. It was a day of disappointment, and although we persevered till darkness closed in upon us, being desperately keen, at last we had to return empty-handed to a spot where the ponies were waiting for us. The burns had been running down all day, and, as soon as I had mounted, my gillie pointed to a ford in front of me, which I proceeded to cross. Just as I got to the opposite bank I heard a cry of distress, and looking round, saw that my unfortunate companion had been dislodged into the water. His pony had shown temper and kicked and bucked in the most inconvenient place. The gillie remarked that it was always nasty if its stable companion was too far ahead of it; a warning which would have

E

been more effectual had it been given before instead of after the catastrophe. His rider was unhurt, and only very little wetter than he had been before; but he preferred to walk the rest of the way, and it was past nine before we got back to the Castle, and nearly midnight before we regained our quarters at Millden. I never remember a longer or harder day, for, although I was in excellent training for walking, I felt the next morning almost as stiff and sore as if I had been beaten with a club.

It was not until many years after that I got my first stag. My lines had fallen in pleasant places, but although every other species of Highland sport had been at my disposal, I had not found a second opportunity of going after the red deer. All comes to him who waits, and at last I found my way to Braemore, the beautiful place of Sir John Fowler. No one but the great engineer, whose achievements in the field of his profession are the pride of his countrymen, could have planned and constructed the sportsman's paradise I then visited for the first time. When he bought his estate in Ross-shire, and considered where to build his house, he determined that it should stand sufficiently high to counteract the somewhat relaxing character of the climate, and should command a view of the strath and of the sea. At once he was assured that no such site existed. But with the giants of his calling there are no such things as impossibilities, and he simply marked on the ordnance map a spot on the side of the hill of the required altitude and situation. As the point selected was on a very steep braeside, 500 feet above the river and the road to Ullapool, it was not desirable to excavate a very large site, and Sir John contented himself with space for his house above, constructing the stables, garden, and offices 500 feet below, with a beautiful winding road of three miles with an easy gradient to connect the two buildings, from the upper of which a stone could almost be dropped upon the other. An unfailing water supply, perfect sanitary arrangements, and power for working machinery and making electric light were provided by damming the burn above and making a little lake close above the house, just below the sanctuary in the heart of the forest below the peaks of Ben Dearig and Ben Lear. The high-road to Garve naturally divides the forest into two beats, and when the wind is in the right quarter, two " rifles " ride together towards the forester's house, and find, if they are in luck, that the stalkers and gillies who have preceded them have spied a stag by the time they reach their several destinations on either side of the highway.

The day contrasted favourably from the outset with the one previously described. The morning was brisk, with just a touch of white frost, and the wind was very nearly due north, and the mist already nearly clear of the highest tops of the hills. As we jogged off together on our stout little Highland ponies, our hearts were light and our hopes high. After we had ridden about three miles my companion turned off to the right across a ford of the river; and two miles farther on I found McHardy, the stalker, and Rory, the forester, intently spying with their glasses at something across the summit-level loch, while their two ponies were feeding by the wayside, and the gillies waiting beside them. Not many words were wasted. As soon as he saw me, McHardy motioned to me to get off my pony, and strode off with my rifle under his arm in the direction of the boat-house, accompanied by one of his myrmidons, after a few Gaelic instructions to the others as to what was to be done with the ponies should fortune favour us. Had I had my present knowledge of his habits I should have augured well from his carrying the rifle, which he never condescended to do unless pretty near the deer. But it was not until we were in the boat and crossing the water that he pointed out to me a rock, not a mile off, where he had discovered a good stag, with some hinds and small beasts, without even leaving the road to go to the usual spying place. We had not had the usual delay and annoyance of having to bale and launch a half-waterlogged boat. On every loch at Braemore the boats are suspended above the water in their houses by an easy arrangement of blocks and pulleys which a child could manage without difficulty. The stalk began soon after we had landed on the other side. The ground was rather flat, and we had to crawl a good deal, and we were delayed more than once by the watchfulness of the sentinel hinds, which raised their heads and stared in our direction, as if they thought there was something amiss, while we, like St. Hilda's fossils, changed for the moment from serpents into stones, and breathed a supplication that we might escape notice. At last we reached a spot where there was no chance of their seeing us, and for a short five minutes I enjoyed the bliss of straightening my back and legs. A crouch and crawl, which could not have lasted a quarter of an hour, although it seemed an age, brought me to a heathery knoll, close under which I believed my stag to be lying; and my belief was changed to a certainty when I saw McHardy take the rifle out of its cover, insert a cartridge, and, beckoning to me to follow, worm himself very slowly and cautiously up the little eminence. My heart thumped audibly as I came in sight of the stag lying down broadside within ninety yards of me with his head up, and after a whispered colloquy I was allowed to shoot at him as he was. A shot, a bound, a moment of sickening suspense, and he disappeared out of sight. Then the glad certainty that the just crawling beast that I saw as I followed in pursuit could not possibly escape, although for caution's sake I rolled it over with another shot.

His head, a pretty little one of nine points, five on the right antler, is before me as I write, so I have no excuse for exaggeration. He scaled a little over fifteen stone clean, and was quite a creditable but not remarkable beast; but he was my first, and I would not exchange those horns for the finest trophy ever made in Germany. Fortune favoured me that day, as I got another rather larger one in the afternoon. But I have already occupied too much space to describe the incidents of this second stalk. As luck would have it, it gave me an experience of a different sort, as the deer were moving, and after a run to cut them off I had a few minutes' wait, and was then told to take the third stag out of a small herd which trotted past. My beast got the bullet fair in the heart, and rolled over stone-dead, after running on for about fifty yards as if nothing had happened.

Most of the above had been written before Sir John Fowler's death, which took place on Sunday, November 20, 1898, after a long illness borne with characteristic patience and fortitude. It may stand as a tribute to the memory of one from whom I received many kindnesses. It is a strange coincidence that on the last day of the stalking season of 1897—the last its owner spent at Braemore—his favourite pony was killed by a curious accident. As the deer was being strapped on to it, it missed its footing on the side of a slippery brae; and as it rolled over the stag's horn penetrated its heart, causing instant death.

CHAPTER V

THE HERDS OF PROTEUS

I WELL remember when I was counsel before a Committee on a railway bill in the House of Commons—a scheme for improving the communication with the West Highlands—the amusement with which I listened to one piece of evidence given on behalf of the promoters. Of course the traffic was to be enormous; "feuing" on a large scale was to cover the barren hills with desirable residences; tons of herrings for the poor and lobsters for the rich were to increase the food-supply of the metropolis; millions of roofing slates from Easedale and Carnbaan were to cover mansions and cottages from Land's End to John o' Groat's; and lastly—and this was what particularly tickled my fancy—it was probable that there would be a large importation of seals from the western lochs and the Hebrides! The witness believed, or let us charitably hope so—at any rate he wished the Committee to believe—that nothing but the want of railway communication prevented the City magnates from supporting native industry by buying the acres of sealskin which covered their own bow-windows, and the even more ample proportions of their wives, from shippers in Argyleshire; and that all danger of a quarrel with America or Russia over disputed rights to the seals at Alaska would come to a natural end by the simple process of the cessation of the demand for the foreign article. Who knows whether, if that abortive scheme had only become law, Reuben Paine and Tom Hall, the heroes of Rudyard Kipling's "Rhyme of the Three Sealers," might not have been alive to this day! I pricked my ears up at once. I did not then know as much about gradients, curves, and engineering difficulties as I do now, but I did know something — perhaps more than any man in the room — about the natural history of the West Coast; and I wondered how many truck-loads of seals were to be brought up to London in the course of the year, and, if any were brought, what in the world would be done with them. Certainly a waistcoat made of pelt of the British seal (*Phoca vitulina*) would look more peculiar than becoming; and although the fishermen and crofters are glad of his blubber for lighting and other purposes, in these days of gas and electric light it would hardly pay to export it to the great metropolis.

I need hardly point out to the intelligent reader that seals, although they are to be found in the West Highlands if you know where to look for them, are not so common as the expert witness appeared to suppose. My personal experience dates back for more than a generation, and although many autumns have been spent in a locality peculiarly favourable for the purpose, the number of seals I have bagged could be counted on the fingers of my two hands. True it is that, as I have grown older, the sporting mania has somewhat yielded to the more humane instincts of the observer and naturalist, and that for some years I have enjoyed watching seals when on my various dredging, yachting, and fishing expeditions without any desire to take their lives. Yet, although I protest against the useless slaughter of any living creature, I cannot hold the killing of seals as unjustifiable, as they are certainly most mischievous and destructive at the mouths of the salmon rivers. Their bodies are covered with a considerable quantity of valuable blubber, and although their pelts are not adapted for the manufacture of mantles and waistcoats, they make excellent gun-covers, or nice mats mounted as sporting trophies. I leave it to others, however, to thin their dwindling numbers, and I should not publish my experiences if I thought I was assisting their destruction by revealing their hiding-places. For various reasons, they shift their ground from time to time, and if any should now visit Loch Craignish in the hope of repeating my successes, they would probably meet with disappointment.

THE HERDS OF PROTEUS

My earliest acquaintance with seals was made in my undergraduate days in the neighbourhood of Valentia, on the west coast of Ireland. There I first saw their round, dog-like heads protruding from the water, and I borrowed a Snider rifle from the coastguard and fired sundry ineffectual shots at them. Finding this unavailing, I next visited the rock cave afterwards described by Trench in his "Reminiscences," and swam in about a hundred yards from the narrow entrance with a lighted candle in my hat and a club swung to my wrist in the hope of finding some seals at rest on the shelving beach at the end, and encountering and vanquishing them in single combat. Looking backwards in the light of experience, I am not so sure that it was to be regretted that the enemy was "not at home"; for, as Monkbarns says, in the "Antiquary," of the *Phoca*, "they bite like furies"; and, attired as I was, in a hat and nothing more, in a place where all retreat from the seals was cut off, I might have come off even worse than Hector M'Intyre did in his celebrated encounter.

When next I saw the seal in his native element the scene had shifted to the west coast of Scotland, and I was one of a party assembled on the rocks at Duntroon, on a very hot Sunday in August 1867. We had been to church in the morning, and had broken the Sabbath in the afternoon by a delicious plunge into the clear water, and were now lazily sunning ourselves on the rock, from which in those days the stake-nets extended far into the bay. There, on the glassy surface, appeared the head of a large seal. We were a somewhat noisy party, and very conspicuous with our white towels, but the seal swam straight towards us, turning neither to the right hand nor to the left. He knew it was Sunday just as well as we did—as almost every kind of wild animal does—and he literally approached within thirty yards of us, and in another minute we could see the corks of the net shaking, as he explored its meshes in the hope of getting a salmon without the trouble of hunting it. This was more than we could stand, and we pelted him with stones till we "made him leave that."

This sight renewed in me the desire to get the skin of a seal of my own killing, and I confided my wish to my good-natured host, then, as always, desirous that every guest should enjoy the sport which pleased him best. The keepers were consulted, and reported that seals in large numbers frequented a rock opposite the Goat Island in Loch Craignish, and that it would not be difficult, by landing on the far side and crawling cautiously to the top, to get a good shot. Three days afterwards the tide was reported to be suitable, and we set sail in the *Troich Dhu* (Black Dwarf), a little half-decked yacht of five tons, with rifles borrowed from our host, determined that this time at least we would obtain the coveted trophy. I do not dwell upon all the incidents of the voyage; suffice it to say that, after a long beat to windward, we duly arrived on the outside of the island, and, after anchoring our little craft, rowed off in the dingey, and effected a cautious and noiseless landing at a somewhat difficult point just opposite the rock where we hoped to find the seals. Should we toss up or draw for first shot? No; that would give but a poor chance to number two, as the seals were not likely to wait for a second barrel. So, after some discussion, we agreed to crawl up side by side, each select a victim, and fire at the word of command—one—two—three. I am not sure, now, that such an arrangement was very likely to be successful, but it was the only means of reconciling the claims of two sportsmen at one and the same stalk. Cautiously we climbed up the steep side, and then, regardless of scratches and running water, crawled along side by side towards the point from which we hoped to obtain an easy shot. We were almost on the sky-line, and in another minute we should have been resting ourselves and selecting our mark, when a portentous bang awoke the echoes for miles around, and we rushed, hoping against hope, to the edge, only to see the rings in the calm water round the rock, which clearly denoted that several seals had actually dived off, and that but for that horrid explosion our manœuvre would have been completely successful. I draw a veil over our sensations as we waited for some time watching the black heads bobbing up, as inquisitive seals asked with inquiring eye why some one had made such a beastly row and disturbed their mid-day siesta. We fired a few random shots at long ranges, but our chance was over for the day, and we returned wrathful and meditating vengeance to find out who or what had spoilt our sport, and whether it had been done by accident or design. Imagine our disgust when we saw Mr. Pender's yacht under sail in the offing, and found out that the skipper had saluted the flag of our little vessel, intending it, in his innocence, as a graceful compliment. Lucky for the crew that we carried no cannon either for purposes of annoyance or defence, or I believe we should have pursued and engaged and sunk them, or perished in the attempt.

Years passed before I secured my first seal. During the interval I shot at their heads from a boat more than once, and sometimes at a reasonable distance; but I never got one. The ball always seemed to strike near them—sometimes I could almost have sworn that I struck the very spot, and tried to persuade myself that I had hit my mark—but I do not really believe I ever shot one. A seal usually makes his appearance when you least expect him, and it is not an easy thing to snatch up your rifle and get a good shot at him before he is down again. If he has been up any time, it is ten to one that he is watching you, and that he will duck the flash; and with both boat and seal in motion it is not easy to take an accurate aim.

However, a day came at last when I fired a successful shot from the gig between Poltalloch farm and Eil-an-righ, and although the seal disappeared, the reddened water showed clearly enough that the shot had struck home. I feared he was lost; but after a few minutes he rose to the surface about sixty yards farther off, and we pursued him in the boat, his dives growing shorter and shorter each time he rose. At last we approached sufficiently near him to drive a long trident-shaped barbed fish-spear into his body, and we had almost got him to the side of the boat when he gave a convulsive struggle, twisted the strong triple barbs almost into the shape of fish-hooks, and once more dropped off into the deep water. I feared that he was lost to me after all, but this was his last effort, and when he rose again we were able to secure him with the spear and lift him on board. The skin was mine at last, but sadly spoiled by the wounds inflicted by the barbs in his struggle to get off.

I pause for a moment in my narrative to discuss the vexed question whether a seal shot in the water invariably sinks. The experience I have just stated is one instance to the contrary; but I should hesitate to dogmatise from a single case, although I think that others, and those often the most positive, are not always equally cautious. I am convinced that it is impossible to lay down any definite rule. I have known a shot seal to sink immediately. I have known one to float for some time and to go down gradually, just disappearing below the surface as the boat got within an oar's length of him; while others have floated for half-an-hour or more, like logs, and have gradually been driven ashore by the wind or tide. I am quite unable to account for the difference. It cannot be the situation or nature of the wound, as it is next to impossible to hit a seal in the water anywhere but in the head, which is the only part exposed. My opinion, for what it is worth, is that it depends upon the condition of the animal's lungs—whether or not they happen at the time to be sufficiently filled with air to float him; but it is always uncertain, and by far the most satisfactory mode of getting a seal is to shoot him on a rock, or else in sufficiently shallow water to make it easy to recover him even in the event of his sinking.

Of course the most exciting sport with seals, as with all other game when it is possible, is a legitimate stalk. To spy your beast from a distance, to make a long détour, making due allowance for wind, approach under cover of rock or bushes, and kill your seal so dead that he never hears the shot that struck him, is sport indeed worthy of the name. The places, however, where seals can be got in this manner are few and far between. They usually choose secluded rocks unapproachable from land, and, sleepy as they look, are off like lightning at the slightest sound of oars or footsteps. I used, however, to know at least two places where at a low spring-tide seals were almost certain to be found reposing on a sunny day, and where I have had several successful expeditions. One was off the mainland, just below the spot where the rugged cairns of Benan tower above Loch Craignish, where a flat rock, only dry at low water, afforded a favourite resting-place for these amphibious creatures, so graceful in the water, so awkward and clumsy-looking on shore. There I have frequently watched, and at least once stalked and secured them; but, until the island opposite was inhabited and the farmhouse occupied, a more sure find was a cluster of long rocks about a hundred yards outside it, which at a suitable tide was almost certain to have quite a colony of amphibious tenants. In that farmhouse nearly a century ago a certain Miss Minnie, a distant connection of the house of Malcolm, had lived and flourished, monarch, not of all she surveyed, for the prospect was somewhat extensive, but at least supreme in her island kingdom. A solitary place, not suited for lovers

F

of society, but not without its attractions and charms for the student of nature. After Miss Minnie's decease, the farmhouse being deserted and the ferry disused, the seals took possession of these rocks on each side, which were far up the loch and seldom disturbed; but recently the farm has been let again with an adjacent island, the house once more echoes with human voices, and the traffic with the mainland is renewed, so the poor seals have been evicted from some of their last refuges without compensation for disturbance.

Dear, beautiful Loch Craignish! How many happy days can I remember on its surface! As Macallum and Sandy pull us round from Duntroon the dredge is on board, and the ladies' sketch-books, as well as a substantial luncheon basket; but it is a low spring-tide, and the ostensible objects of our expedition are seals and oysters. The latter, alas! are now few and far between, but some may be secured at dead low water sticking to the rocks, and, if so, what an addition they will make to our lunch! No germs of typhoid can lurk in the clear sea water, and one old fellow has five times as much flesh on him as the degenerate Native of the South, and three times as much flavour. On we go, inside Rabbit Island, past the point of Ardifure, and round under the shore of Macaskan, still inhabited by fallow-deer, with one solitary shepherd and his family to look after them. Sandy, the youngest of our boatmen, is in his own country now, for he is a son of that very herd; and many a morning have he and his brother and sister crossed the loch, and tramped two miles across the hill on their way to the school at Kilmartin, a sample of that energy in pursuit of knowledge under difficulties which accounts for the superior education of the Scotch in bygone days. Next we pass the unused limekiln, which the ladies formerly used as a dressing-room when enjoying a dip—one, I remember, complained bitterly of a cow having fallen into her dressing-room—and so on past Goat Island (no longer a haunt of seals) to Eil-an-righ. As we pass along, the fern and the ripening rowan berries glitter in the sun, the buzzard soars round the peak above, heron and gull flap lazily past, and screaming terns hover and plunge into the water, rising with glittering herring fry in their beaks. Curlews and oyster-catchers run along the shores, and the hooded crows too are busy among the seaweed. Cormorants spread out their wings, drying themselves on the rocks; while we are accompanied by a perfect convoy of guillemots, swimming and diving around us fearless of harm. More than one seal has shown his head within shot of us, and after a prolonged stare lifted his nose in the air and disappeared, to break the water again perhaps three hundred yards off, perhaps a mile; but we are not tempted to fire till we have explored the rocks. The glassy surface looks as if it could never be ruffled, but appearances are deceptive, and it is not a nice place to be attempted by unskilled boatmen or with a fastened sheet. Like all Highland lochs under high hills, it is very subject to squalls, which sweep down with extraordinary suddenness and great violence. But our boatmen are both capable and cautious; to-day, however, there is no need for their skill or care, for we pursue our course under a sapphire sky till we reach the landing-place at Eil-an-righ. Some of the party stop by the beautiful spring, in its nest of hart's-tongue and lady-fern, surrounded by boulders covered with moss and hymenophyllum, while I and two of the ladies go up the path to spy the rocks. No need of caution here, as we are more than half a mile off, so we seat ourselves on a boulder and carefully spy. Sure enough there are four seals on the nearest rock: one or two wriggling and twisting their heads and tails round in awkward and ungainly attitudes, one large dark fellow lying perfectly still with his head turned towards the shore. I carefully mark the exact spot, and, leaving the others to watch, take my single-barrelled Henry out of its case and start off on my stalk. It is easy enough to get within three hundred yards. Up to that point I have shelter, and cover of rock, hazel, and birch; but just below are a flock of wild ducks, and if I put them up good-bye to my seals. Another round and I come to a little burn, which finds its way into the sea just at the nearest point to the seal rock. It is wet, it is slippery, it is uncomfortable, but no matter—I crawl along, often in a pool of water, till I find myself at a point hardly more than a hundred yards from my objective. I pause to take breath, then slowly and cautiously raise my head. There they are still, and my dark friend is motionless in the same attitude. I rest my left hand on the rock, my rifle on my left hand, take a steady aim, and pull. There is a smoke, a splash, several splashes, as the seals flop heavily into the water, but, when the smoke clears away, my dark friend is still lying there in the same attitude, absolutely motionless, a thin stream of blood flowing from his throat just below the nose. The ball has caught him fair this time, and his skin is mine. Splashing, sliding, and jumping, I find my way across the sand and boulders through the shallow water; but there is no need to hurry—the dark seal never moves again.

After this success oysters sound an unromantic object of pursuit; but we get a few, and enjoy them as a relish to our picnic. The seal is handed over to Hugh Gillies, the herd, to skin, and he is well pleased to do it, as the flesh and blubber become his perquisite. I should not care to eat seal myself, but Esquimaux like it, and Macallum and Sandy assure me it is very like veal.

We dredge with varied success while the skinning is going on, and then, as a light breeze springs up, for once from the right quarter, we return home under sail. Behind us, as we turn into Loch Crinan, the sky over the whirlpool between Jura and Scarba is flooded with molten gold and purple, and the sun has sunk behind the islands before our party lands, after a day for ever to be marked with a white stone.

CHAPTER VI[1]

A DAY WITH A SEAL

IT is no part of my intention, speaking without authority and with little experience, to discuss seriously the ethics of seal-shooting. In spite of every natural advantage with which a careful Providence has supplied them, the numbers of these animals in most localities are rapidly diminishing, and a logical encouragement of their destruction could serve no good purpose whatever; while, having fairly won as good a trophy as that which adorns the room in which I am writing, I feel it is unlikely that I shall join in the persecution of seals on any future occasion.

I have been carefully brought up to believe in the rough classification of the objects of sport under two heads—animals useful for food or other purposes when dead, and animals which do mischief when alive; and I am ready to admit that it would be sophistical to include seals nowadays under either category, for the useful blubber is

---

[1] This chapter is by my son Geoffrey. I have included it in this volume because it describes the sport of seal stalking in another locality, and from a somewhat different point of view.

seldom saved by the natives whose perquisite it becomes; and where seals are mischievous, they have already been proportionately exterminated, while, though I have eaten the meat, and should have no objection whatever to doing so again, I hardly think that the practice is sufficiently general to admit of the classification of *Phoca vitulina* as a table delicacy.

But when we look further afield and see that those animals which offer the most irresistible attractions to the sporting instinct, such, for example, as the ibex or the chamois, would arouse neither the enthusiasm of the epicure nor the enmity of the gamekeeper, we may surely confess that there may be exceptions to a generally useful rule, and that the difficulties and discomforts incidental to the stalking of certain creatures may serve alone as the sportsman's excuse for coveting their trophies. If, therefore, in accurately describing a day on an island (which shall be nameless) where seals are in no danger of extinction, I can show these qualifications to have existed, I hope I shall at least escape a hasty classification as an extremely pernicious variety of the degraded genus "gull-plugger."

It is a fine September morning. Not a breath of wind moves the tops of the trees which shelter the house; everything promises a thoroughly broiling day. I come down to breakfast animated by a hope that no stern parental fiat will

A DAY WITH A SEAL

drive me perspiring after the sparsely sprinkled grouse which my unvarying inaccuracy with the fowling-piece has left upon the small but vicious steeps of the island. The warm sun and still air are certain to tempt a considerable number of seals to bask for most of the day on the reefs of Ardskinish, or the rocks to the south of it, and I mean to stalk and secure one before the day is many hours older. Moreover, to-morrow is a post-day, so that I shall be able to send the skin at once to be dressed if I am fortunate in my efforts. There are two post-days in the week, a preposterous number in the eyes of the local postman, which he generally contrives by self-instituted holidays to reduce to more reasonable proportions.

Very shortly after breakfast I am under way with a telescope in its case, lunch in a bag on my shoulders, and a small ·250 American rifle in my hand. This weapon is not for the benefit of the seals, though I firmly believe it would answer well enough, but for any rabbits or other small game which I may encounter in the course of the four miles which are before me, or later in the day, if fortune favours my main object early. As I pass through the gates of the carriage drive I come in view of a field which almost invariably contains a few black game, and there, sure enough, is an old cock about a hundred and twenty yards from me, but barely fifty from the buckthorn hedge which bounds the field on the home side. Cautiously I slip back and sneak along the hedge, but the wily old bird has witnessed that manœuvre before, and is off, having either heard or seen me before my stalk has proceeded very far. However, I shall no doubt pursue him or one of his relations with better success another day, so I regard his flight with considerable equanimity and resume my course along the road.

A couple of unsuccessful shots have completely destroyed my bottle-born confidence—pray do not be shocked, the bottle was empty, and a hundred yards from my rifle barrel—by the time that I have covered about three miles and come up with the dog-cart, where my ·303 rifle is awaiting me in charge of my sister, who has expressed a wish to accompany me on my stalk as far as is possible without risk of putting off my game, as she is anxious to see seals alive or dead at closer quarters than she has hitherto succeeded in attaining. The other occupants of the dog-cart are two incurable golfo-maniacs. One of the miserable victims of this insidious complaint claims my sympathy in deference to the Fifth Commandment. He is not yet in the acute or solitary stage which drives a man to dig divots from his carpet with a mashie, and break his furniture with (so-called) captive golf-balls, but his behaviour in the presence of

A DAY WITH A SEAL

another sufferer makes me fear the worst. For the past week he has deserted the moor, and here he will be found to-day, as usual, gazing reproachfully at the rabbit-hole down which eighteenpence worth of gutta-percha has just vanished, or vainly endeavouring to impress on the uninitiated youth of the island the subtle distinction between a putter and a mashie. But I will dwell no further on this piteous spectacle. Let us pass on.

Another mile brings us to our first spying ground—a narrow rocky pass in the hill overlooking the promontory of Ardskinish. Here I remove from my pockets any things which are liable to be spoilt by contact with sea water, and placing them in the lunch-bag, deposit the latter on the ground for the present with my rabbit rifle in a cover beside it. Then seating myself on a convenient stone, I take out my glass and proceed to spy for seals.

A more dreary spot than Ardskinish it has seldom been my misfortune to see. A line of low sand dunes clothed in hard grey bents is protected from the force of the Atlantic by a most inhospitable reef, almost entirely submerged at high tide. A lighthouse just visible on the horizon, far out to sea, is the last vestige of land between these rocks and the Western Hemisphere. To the usefulness of this light the islanders give a valuable testimonial from a somewhat grimly original point of view, "It's just spoilin' the place for wrecks!" Yet to the eye of an ordinary landsman the shore is plentifully strewn with masts, spars, and broken timbers, while long bamboo canes and fragments of larger trees than the islands produce testify to the proximity of the Gulf Stream. A small farmhouse partially concealed by intervening dunes completes the picture.

But to-day this picture is all that greets the eye, and the telescope reveals no shining backs or wriggling hind-flippers on that piece of the reef which is visible from our present point of view. Accordingly, we move on to the dunes themselves till we reach a place whence a more likely part of the low, weed-covered rocks can be spied, and here, unless I am very much mistaken, we must find our game. And so it turns out, for after one or two sweeps the movement of the glass is arrested by a dark object waving above a rock against the bright background of sea beyond. A second glance confirms what experience has told me, that what I saw was the tail and hind-flippers of a seal, and in another moment I have counted five, lying on a small rock whose weed-covered top is only just clear of the calm water. It will mean a swim for the body, if the shot is successful, for the little island is at some distance from the main reef, but a thorough wetting is the inevitable accompaniment

A DAY WITH A SEAL

of a crawl over these low rocks with their multitude of intersecting channels, and I have never brought myself within range of seals, either to watch and sketch them, or when acting as stalker for a friend, without being pretty consistently moistened throughout.

Certainly no one could reasonably object to seal-shooting on grounds of humanity. Lying as these animals do so near to the water that one kick will probably carry the coveted skin to a depth whence it would usually be impossible to regain it, there is no temptation to the most unsportsmanlike to aim anywhere but at the brain, and this with ordinary luck entails instantaneous death or entire immunity to the quarry.

Between me and the five seals which I have just discovered there are some high rocks where sand leaves off and reef begins, to which both I and my sister have no difficulty whatever in attaining. Beyond them, however, there is promise of an unusually flat crawl before a point can be reached at which a shot would be reasonable, and I have a very vivid anticipation of the effect of the "juts of pointed rock" which will shortly be searching out the tenderest portions nominally protected beneath a sodden waistcoat during my serpentine progress towards the desired goal.

Behind the friendly shelter of the high rocks I leave therefore the passive spectator with my glass. My course lies first through a large rock pool, quite shallow from an ordinary point of view, but, as it has to be traversed at a flat crawl, I emerge ready for any depth of sea above which I can manage to hold the rifle, which I am carrying still in its cover.

And now, after worming my way for some yards along a very slight dip in the rocks, mercifully coated with soft seaweed, I come to perhaps the most critical point in the difficult stalk before me. The necessity of keeping out of sight has led me some distance almost at right angles to the direct line between the high rocks and the game, to a spot whence I can return along a channel which is fortunately almost empty at this state of the tide, and thereafter pursue a straighter and more rapid course. But the channel has first to be entered, and, though I have chosen the only practicable point, yet flatten myself how I will, some part of my clothing, which is fortunately of an excellent colour for concealment, must for a moment come into sight of the seals as I drop over the nearer edge of the hollow.

And, indeed, just as I am blessing my stars for the safe accomplishment of a ticklish manœuvre, down come most of the waving hind-flippers, up go all the dark shiny heads, and one great brute gives himself a shove off which nearly lands him in the water. He fortunately hesitates on the brink, and after some moments of agonising suspense, during which I dare not breathe,

A DAY WITH A SEAL

while the rock beneath my waistcoat seems to possess a hundred extra and unaccountable angles, all the seals drop their heads once more, regarding me as a curious seismic phenomenon, or regretting the rash and inconsiderate haste with which their last meal was devoured. Fortunately, I am so nearly across that as soon as I am no longer the cynosure of ten amphibious eyes I can drop unostentatiously into the comparative shelter of the channel.

Creeping back along this, I come once more into an almost direct line between the starting-point and the goal, and here, though the far side of the channel no longer shelters me, the low rocks slope slightly upwards to the spot whence I hope to take my shot. It is merely a question of imitating the progress of the worm for a short time longer. Vain hope! After going forward some distance I find that the desired firing-point is separated from me by a strait of sea which the intervening reef has concealed hitherto from eyes kept down close to the surface of the rocks. Well, there is no other way. I must slip into the sea on my right, and trust that the rock will hide from the eyes of the seals as much of my person as must be kept above the water. Having taken the cover from my rifle, since the goal does not promise much shelter for movements of the kind, I slip in a cartridge, and let my feet down into the sea. Fortune is favourable, and with my face bent almost to the level of the calm water I succeed in wading across without mishap, and sliding my arms and rifle on to the rock raise my head slowly, and lie with a feeling of relief within range of the game, most of the lower half of my body still resting merman-like in another element.

There are the seals, basking without suspicion, and as I watch another swims up and joins them. They lie, not as in most pictures they are represented, with heads up and tails down, breasts to the rocks, but in every variety of attitude.

Most are on their sides, looking like great slugs, an occasional lazy wriggle being their only sign of life, save when a fore-flipper is raised in vigorous assault upon one of those parasites from which an amphibious existence does not appear to protect the genus. A friend of mine once irreverently applied the phrase "a land in which it seemed always after lunch" to a seal-haunted rock, and certainly a group of basking seals is irresistibly suggestive of the lotus-eaters.

Two of the group before me offer good targets as they lie, but they seem to be small, and I can make out brown patches of old hair which spoil the appearance of the skin. The best from every point of view is lying tail on to me

A Seal-haunted rock.

A DAY WITH A SEAL

with his head held low and hidden behind the line of his broad back. However, better no seal at all than a bad one, so I must wait until he raises his head. This he seems inclined to take his time about, though while I was stalking he seemed ready enough to have obliged me in this respect had I wished it. At last, however, three parts of a small circle rise above the line of his back, and, aiming carefully, I squeeze the trigger.

Crack! splash! splash! the water round the rock is disturbed, and four seals have vanished, but my friend has resumed his old position with his head hidden from view, and will not move again.

"Accoutred as I was," except for my coat, of which I have hastily divested myself, I dash into the sea and swim across, while my sister comes from her hiding-place towards the scene, as far as it is possible to pick a comparatively dry way.

But, alas! the disasters of the day are only now about to begin. As soon as, grasping the seal by the hind-flippers, I have dragged it out of my depth, it sinks by the head, and my swimming powers, though sufficient as I know to have dragged the dead beast lengthwise over the sea, are not equal to overcoming the resistance offered to the water by the whole of the body, particularly as that resistance acts only on the side of the hand which is holding the flippers. So after a short struggle I am compelled to take the corpse for the present back to its rock again.

And now it strikes me that shooting-boots of gigantic size are hardly conducive to good swimming, so I take them off, and, tying them together by the laces, start back again, holding them in one hand.

> "But oftentimes to win us to our harm,
> The instruments of darkness tell us truths,"

and though I swim with greater ease and rapidity, better would it have been had I persisted in the old arrangement. As I near the spot whence I fired, the particular "instrument of darkness" who rules the destinies of this fatal day unties the knot, and a wild clutch only succeeds in rescuing one useless foot covering from a watery grave! At such a depth it needs a better diver than myself to recover its fellow.

I go off as fast as bootless feet can carry me over the sharp rocks, to a point on the beach where I remember to have seen a bough of conderable length lying among the other driftwood and wreckage. With this and with the lunch I return, and we spend much valuable time in just failing to reach the lost boot with the extempore grappling-hook. The clear water shows it tantalisingly near—in fact, so well can I see it that, as we cease our vain attempts, the crabs sur-

A DAY WITH A SEAL

rounding and entering its recesses are distinctly visible.

But time and tide wait neither for the rescue of boots nor for the devouring of sandwiches, and the rising water threatens shortly to wash the dead seal from its rock. What is to be done? There is no time to skin him where he lies. Off I rush again, across the rocks, across the dunes, the bents and thistles stabbing at my bootless feet, to ask at the farm for a rope, which may enable me to drag the body by the heavy end, and thus get rid of a considerable part of the resistance to the water; though, of course, my ideal is a rope long enough to reach the whole of the distance between the seal's rock and the land. A woman comes out in response to my knock; the rest of the inhabitants are elsewhere, working in the corn. After she has overcome her surprise at my appearance, as I stand dripping in stockings and shirt sleeves, she offers me refreshment, which I decline, and then goes to search for rope, returning after a considerable interval with a few short odds and ends of doubtful-looking cordage, with which I am obliged with thanks and apologies to depart.

Returning to the reef, I hastily break off as much of the rope as is too rotten to stand a moderate strain, and, connecting the rest, swim once again to the body, which the water is by this time actually touching.

Here I fasten a loop firmly round the beast behind the fore-flippers, and taking a turn of the other end of the rope round my right hand, enter the water again.

For a while all goes well, and I am complimenting myself on the final conclusion of my labours, when suddenly I feel the touch of the rope against my instep. Unwilling to be entangled, I pause to let the slack sink out of my way, and having accomplished this object resume my former rate. But, alas! I had forgotten a secondary result of this manœuvre. As the rope comes taut again there must necessarily be a jerk —yes, sure enough, the jerk takes place, and the next moment I find myself swimming on with a yard and a half of rotten hemp in my hand. The rope was broken, and my seal has sunk where I cannot hope to reach him, has foundered in fact within sight of port! There are feelings too deep for words, and, besides, there is a lady present. So silently and gloomily I leave Ardskinish, and my "damp unpleasant body" is soon being whirled home on the back seat of a buckboard, a part of that ingenious vehicle which is not conducive at the best of times to a pleasant frame of mind— but now!

The next day we return with grappling-hooks and no ladies, and my brother, a more skilful diver than myself, prepares to perform in the costume or want of it best adapted to success;

A DAY WITH A SEAL

but the weather has changed, it is bitterly cold, the transparence of yesterday's sea is broken by wind and rain, and though the bottom is searched at various points, that seal, my boot, and the farmer's ropes are never seen again!

However, perseverance is eventually rewarded, and, in the evening of the Saturday following the disaster, a short stalk earned me a successful shot at a good seal, whose body, carried with difficulty to a safe place, 1 was, owing to various mistakes and misunderstandings, compelled to leave for the night. The next day being Sunday, to ask for native assistance in Sabbatarian Scotland was, of course, as out of the question as to leave the body to the mercy of rats and gulls. Accordingly, in the afternoon I and my brother might have been seen on the road to Ardskinish, both of us attired in our oldest clothes, whilst an unusual protuberance of my coat in the region of my chest testified to the presence of a sack beneath it. Arrived at the spot we carried the body aside, and although a seal is not so easy to flay as most animals, as the skin will not come away from the blubber without the constant use of a knife, in course of time the deed was done, and we returned home with the skin in a sack, oily, but triumphant. Indirectly we were the gainers, for the natives almost always cut the flippers off, whereas we skinned them conscientiously, and thus even the claws were preserved. And now as I write, the beautifully dappled trophy, almost as long as its owner, is proudly displayed upon the floor before me to remind me of the difficulties and catastrophes which ended in its attainment; and which, with the excitement incidental to the pursuit of an animal so well protected both by its senses and its surroundings, may perhaps go far to palliate, if not to justify, an occasional day with a seal.

CHAPTER VII

OUT OF THE DEPTHS

THE West Coast of Scotland has a bad reputation, as having a damp climate; but, in spite of almanacs and rain-gauges, I believe it has been slandered. In all the autumns I have spent there, I have seldom known it to rain quite enough. Truth compels me to own that I may be prejudiced, as I am an enthusiastic fisherman, and the little river where I love to spend my holidays runs up and down in a few hours, and requires a constant succession of "spates" to keep it in order. All, however, must agree that when you do get a really fine day in Argyleshire nothing can be more lovely than the mixture of sea and sky, colour and shadow, that can be seen from the hill-tops. As far as the horizon, land and sea, peak and promontory, stretch out, intersecting one another, so that any one not well acquainted with the country would be puzzled to know which is island and which is mainland, or to realise that what appear to be lakes are really undivided from the broad Atlantic. On the north can be distinguished the bold outline of Ben Cruachan, clear, but faint, in the distance. Loch Awe is between it and the spectator, but is hidden in the valley. To the north-west, over the round hill of Scarba, stand out the blue mountains and bold cliffs of Mull. Straight to the west, across the point of Craignish, is the whirlpool of Corrievreken and the northern point of Jura, while a little more to the south her high double peaks are a conspicuous object. South-east, the whole length of Loch Fyne can be seen as far as Arran. Numerous rocks and smaller islands also show themselves in every direction, while dark lines of tangle or white breakers tell their tale of sunken reefs, which, with those in sight, make this coast a dangerous one to the inexperienced navigator.

The sea is always a subject for ridicule with comic versifiers, and the torments of sea-sickness an unvarying source of amusement to shilling galleries or music-hall audiences. Lewis Carroll has his

> "Vision of nursery maids,
> Tens of thousands passed by me,
> All leading children with wooden spades,
> And this was by the sea.
>
> . . . . .
>
> Pour some salt water over the floor,
> Ugly I'm sure you'll allow it to be;
> Suppose it extended a mile or more,
> That's very like the sea."

When this is his description, it is no wonder that the sea should be the pet object of his detestation; but for my part there is something in the splash of the waves, the rise and fall of the tide, the smell of the salt, which reconciles me even to the bathing-machines, the long monotonous frontage, the negro minstrels, the Salvation Army, the organ-grinders, the shrimp-sellers, and the whole posse comitatus of a fashionable watering-place. Judge then of my delight in a sea not bearing the remotest resemblance to the satirist's caricature—a sea which, at the rise and fall of the tide, rushes and eddies round innumerable rocks and islands, whirling and roaring like a mill-race at the rate of eight or nine knots an hour—a sea as clear as a Hampshire trout-stream, the calm recesses of which the eye may penetrate to a depth that I am afraid to state in figures for fear I should be accused of exaggeration. There, as you hang over the side of the boat, you may see the long lazy tangle waving its broad streamers over the dark rocks, the fish darting about among the undergrowth, the comical crabs parading, fighting, and gormandising at the bottom; and sea-urchins, from great red fellows as big as a good-sized melon, called seal's eggs by the natives, to little ones no bigger than a walnut, which, in some places, literally pave the sand, and render it rather an uncomfortable pavement for bare-footed children, who endeavour to emulate the feats of Margate or Hastings on its prickly surface. Every pool left by the tide is full of corallines and beautiful anemones, and the shore hunter may gather a rich harvest by turning the stones, digging in the sand, or examining the sea-weed—a harvest of "common objects" here, some of them by no means common in the eye of an experienced naturalist or collector. But we must no longer loiter on the shore. "Out of the Depths" is my subject, and I am longing for a turn at my favourite pursuit, and must start without further delay to explore with the dredge the mysterious depths of this bright and bewitching sea for the treasures which may lurk among its crowded hollows, at a depth of twenty to thirty fathoms. It is always as well to have a direct object in view, and to-day I am in search especially of the sea-rush (*Virgularia mirabilis*), a rare and mysterious compound polyp, to be found in these latitudes, either in the neighbourhood of the West Coast or in the adjoining Irish loughs. I have found it before, and know that friends at the British Museum would be glad to have the opportunity of examining living specimens, in view of some of those problems which yet await solution at the hands of the ardent collector, an honour which may—who knows?—fall to myself, perhaps this very day.

It is high time we were off, but I must not forget my pensioners, the paupers, as they are contemptuously termed—the black-headed laughing gulls, which come to be fed every morning after breakfast on the lawn outside the library window. Before I have begun to whistle twenty at least are flying all round me; and they are down upon the grass, fighting for the sopped toast and fishes' heads before I have emptied the bowl of scraps which have been saved for their breakfast from ours. Certainly, in this open weather they no longer require the charity which, in time of winter snow and frost, first brought them to our door, but even if it impairs their moral fibre, we cannot resist feeding them still. I linger a short time, watching one greedy fellow choking over a large bone, and another nicknamed Cross-patch who, with outstretched neck and ruffled feathers, tries to drive his companions away; and then start hurriedly for Duntroon, with my pea-rifle on my shoulder. A fresh north-westerly breeze is blowing, and a few white clouds are hurriedly chasing one another across the blue sky, and telling rather of the shower of last night than promising rain for to-day. The glass *is* rising—not has been rising. There is an important distinction here. Some say you should never trust the glass on the West Coast, but this is incorrect. You should watch it narrowly, and then it is just as truthful as elsewhere, although the changes are more rapid. Your confidence, however, should not be blind; stop your ears to the voice of the aneroid singing—

> "Trust me not at all
> Or trust me all in all,"

and take your waterproof and plenty of wraps, especially if you are going to spend a whole day with me in an open boat, many miles from home or effectual shelter.

As I pass through the wood a beautiful roebuck stares at me within twenty yards, without a sign of fear, although a touch of the trigger could not fail to make his graceful horns my own. His confidence is not misplaced; he is as safe from fire-arms as a fox in Leicestershire, as long as he chooses to remain in this sanctuary, the wood round the house. Next, as I turn down towards the first lodge, a squirrel, his bushy tail almost white, runs across the path, and sits up watching me without dropping the large bit of red fungus which he is carrying in his mouth. Him, perhaps, I ought to kill, for I have passed some tell-tale shoots of ornamental pine on the path which remind me that my little friend is as mischievous as he is pretty; but, if he must die, others may shoot him, not I. I decline to be his executioner; but I should be sorry to insure his life if my schoolboy son happened to pass him rifle in hand. Anything good to eat or mischievous is his legitimate prey;

but he has been taught to spare the graceful sea-fowl and comical cormorants, and to look upon a "gull-plugger"—a race, alas! not extinct even in the West Highlands—with contempt and aversion. On I go, along the road by the shore, picking up a few rabbits on my way, leaving some at the lodges and carrying two or three along for the boatmen; and watching the beautiful shaggy-fronted Highland cattle, so terrible in their appearance to Southron nursemaids, so harmless and peaceable in reality, as they wade far out into the water to get away from the flies; while curlews, oyster-catchers, and lapwings run along the sand, filling the air with their musical cries.

Soon Duntroon Castle, the oldest inhabited castle in Scotland, is reached. It is truly founded upon a rock, and has defied the winter storms of many a hundred years, which must have been fatal to anything built on less solid foundations. The boatmen are there, waiting at the gate, to carry down the sea-water jar, the bait-can, the bottles, the wraps, and last, not least, a capacious luncheon-basket; and the sound of wheels behind me announces the arrival of the remainder of the crew, with those useful and necessary articles. There are the children and their companions, and Punch, a little wiry-haired terrier, who would have dearly loved to have accompanied me on foot, instead of coming in the waggonette; and now gives vent to excruciating shrieks and howls of delight at the sight of the rifle and its proprietor. He had to be left behind, because his zeal for sport so far outruns his discretion, that the raising of a gun or rifle is the signal for an outburst which sends every rabbit for miles around scuttling into the safe recesses of the cairns.

The gig, with the dredge on board and two small oars as well as the regular ones, is ready for us, and we are soon all on board, as it would take far too long to beat round to our destination in the large sailing-boat with this north-west wind. The "Pirate King," a young gentleman of eight—so called partly from his nautical costume, blue knitted guernsey and fisherman's cap, and partly because, in his own estimation, he commands the boat—takes the stroke oar, and his sister is No. 3, while the two boatmen settle down to their work in the bows. I am steering at present, but ready to relieve either of the volunteers at a moment's notice; but they will stick to their places for the greater part of the four miles we have to go, and help the boat along, and be too much occupied to feel uncomfortable if there should happen to be a little jobble where wind and tide meet. On we go, past Port-na-Dewar, with its great cliff covered with birch and rowan, and its jackdaw-haunted cairn; past Ardifure, with its snug farm and banks of hazel; past the rabbit island and round into the loch; then away past the islands of Macaskan and Eil-na-gore and almost to Eil-an-righ. On our right is the beautiful bold outline of Benan, its precipitous sides scarred here and there where some great boulder has lately broken away and bounded down the side to join the "tumbled fragments of the hills" which lie below the brae, of all sizes and shapes.

At length we have reached our destination, and it is time to get the dredge overboard. One end of the rope is fastened to a seat, and the other to the dredge—a common oyster dredge of about two-feet beam, with a stout twine net, with a one-inch mesh, instead of the usual iron chain netting. This I find best for my work on this rocky shore. While one man is making ready the dredge, the other fastens between the front seats a large bag of waterproof sail-cloth, in shape something like one of those receptacles into which hop-pickers strip the bine of its blossom. This is destined to hold the contents of the dredge, to be turned over and searched by plenty of willing hands, while itself is making another tour of discovery at the bottom of the loch.

Over it goes with a splash, and Punch would have been in after it if he had not been caught by the collar. That officious little person thinks nothing can be done properly without his help; but although he can swim like a duck, and dive also well enough to get stones and ginger-beer bottles out of the shallows of the Serpentine, he could hardly recover the dredge, which is now rapidly nearing the bottom, at a depth of about thirty fathoms. The men settle to their oars, as there is not breeze enough in this sheltered place to-day to make it worth while to set the sail; and at all times it is difficult to go too slow when dredging. It is hard work while it lasts, but it will not last long, as the net is sure to be full of something before it has gone over more than twenty-five yards of the bottom.

One hand on the rope, just to see that it is keeping on the bottom, and that it does not come to an anchor on some inconvenient boulder, and there is time to look about. There seems to be an unusual commotion in the neighbourhood of the narrow promontory of Macaskan, just opposite, and all the cattle are collected on the shore. All —no, not all; for now we can see what is going on—a line of men and dogs is gathering them there, no doubt to drive them into the sea to swim across the half-mile of water which separates them from the mainland, a first stage on their journey to Falkirk Tryst. What a scene of life and animation! What shouts of men, what barking of collies! What excitement as one great stupid beautiful beast breaks away again and again, carrying with him, by the force of bad example, two or three of his more docile companions, to be headed back again and again by the sagacious collies, who are off round him at a word or a sign from their masters, with a precision astounding to any one who does not recognise the intellect—I will not call it the instinct—of a Scotch sheep-dog. But we must be getting up the dredge; the cattle will not be in the water yet for a bit, and we shall have ample time to see them swim across after the haul has been secured. Now, then, lift away, all together, and up it comes, three pairs of eager eyes straining over the side as the seemingly interminable rope is gradually coiled in the boat.

We have got something; that is quite evident from the weight; and I try to hope, as usual, for some novel and hitherto undiscovered crustacean or starfish, while experience and reason enable me to hazard a pretty good guess of what is really coming. At last the dredge is in sight, and there is no long trail of white mud, no dark tangle; so, as I expected, this time we must have been over hard bottom mixed with shells. One more lift, and the haul is on board and speedily emptied into the bag—one great, brilliant, fourteen-rayed sun-star slipping off the outside of the mesh just as the iron appears over the side. "All right, old fellow; good-bye! We don't want you; and if we did, there are plenty more where you came from."

The catch is heavy enough, but it appears as if there were nothing but bushels of "King

Harrys," the scallop of the pilgrim, and the pincushion, of various hues, red, yellow, brown speckled, and light; and with them a writhing mass of hairy, brittle starfish, many of whom have already contrived to part with some of their limbs in that loose and careless fashion which characterises many marine species, their own above all others. Throw the brittle starfish overboard, and put the largest of the "King Harrys" into the basket; they are excellent, scalloped or curried; but the small ones may go back, for there will be many more than we can require for any purpose before the day is over. Gradually the heap diminishes, and other creatures begin to make their appearance—pretty swimming crabs, nicknamed velvet fiddlers, their hind-claws flattened into a paddle; and queer, slow-moving spider-crabs, making up by craft for their want of agility, for they have dressed themselves up, one with seaweeds, and another with sponges and live ascidians, so that when not in motion they can hardly be distinguished from the bottom of the sea, and any confiding creatures which come within their reach are apt to discover too late that the seemingly inanimate objects have long claws and healthy appetites. It is most amusing to watch one of these crabs in confinement, combing the seaweed on his back like a gentleman parting his hair. My children christened one the Grand Old Man; why, I cannot imagine, as he did not bear the most distant resemblance to the distinguished statesman who was usually known by that title. Spider-crabs are of different sizes and shapes, and many species are common here, some with scarcely any body and very long and attenuated legs, some clothed, some bare, some great, and some small. Next we see a large red-coloured hermit-crab, looking stupid and unprotected, with its soft, flabby, degenerate tail, no longer covered by a stolen shell. Search the now diminished heap, and the home he has abandoned in his fright will soon be found. There it is, an empty whelk-shell, covered completely over with a curious soft lilac-spotted garment, the cloak anemone, which is also in an excited state, as appears by the long, thread-like lilac acontia which protrude from its spots. Put it into the sea-water bottle, and the hermit with it; with what alacrity he darts back into his house, and closes the front door with his large right claw! The two thieving rogues are united at once—both quite at home, one inside and the other outside the shell manufactured by its original proprietor for its own exclusive use and convenience. Surely there are few more curious creatures than this parasitic anemone, never found except on a whelk shell, and one inhabited by a hermit crab, upon which it is dependent, as it soon dies if deprived of its companion by desertion or death. Why,

I do not exactly know; whether it yearns for carriage exercise or the leavings of a crab's food, but the fact is undoubted, and it is the delicacy of the hermit crab that makes the cloak anemone so difficult a creature to keep in confinement. There is another, a rarer and more beautiful parasitic anemone, which also lives upon the outside of shells, specimens of which I have taken near this very spot; but it seems to prefer long spiral shells, and, although it selects inhabited hermitages, does not insist upon dying of grief or starvation if the original usurper relinquishes possession. I have kept and admired these for months, living on empty shells, and returned them to the sea alive and flourishing at the end of my holiday.

I have not half exhausted the description of my haul, although by no means a first-rate or exceptional one; but it is time to turn round and have another look at the cattle; so I will leave the description of the numerous starfish, tube-worms and smaller creatures for another dredge. There is nothing here that I am not pretty sure to get again before the day is over. There are all the beasts, black, red, and dun, collected on the spit of land nearest to the water with a line of men and dogs behind them. Splash! In goes the first, and the rest soon follow, boldly enough, when once they have made up their minds. Two or three of the dogs pursue them into the sea, and half-a-dozen boats are soon launched behind them, those of the crew who are not rowing, splashing with long green boughs and shouting. How low the cattle swim in the water! there is nothing visible but a forest of horns. Every now and then one attempts to turn, and the excitement is renewed; but as they get farther from the island these attempts to break back become less and less frequent, although the herd still requires guiding, and the pace becomes slower and slower. When the opposite shore is sighted, the course at once becomes straight and the pace improves, and soon I can see, with a glass, first one and then another land and shake himself dry upon the shore, till all are safe on *terra firma*. All the time they are crossing they make a strange blowing sound, like that of a porpoise, and they are evidently frightened at first, as on landing they gallop away from the collies into such rough ground that the dogs are called off and a man sent round to drive them carefully and cautiously into the pass; soon, however, they are going across the hill out of our sight, at a quiet jog-trot pace, and we may resume our dredging.

This time, when the dredge comes up, there is more mud in it, and fewer shells, although it is easy to see by the writhing motion that there is plenty of life in the grey, sticky deposit. A good deal is allowed to be washed away before it comes on board, but slowly and cautiously, as if we were gold-washers with their cradle, and in much the same manner, for it was about here that we last secured the rare creature of which we are now in search; and it is just in this soft sort of ground that it is usually found. A shout of joy and triumph issues from the mouth of the youngest of the party, as he produces a very small reddish object about the thickness of a piece of worsted, and not more than three inches long, in which he has recognised a sea-rush; and I have already got hold of a larger specimen some nine inches long, but, as I am going to explain, not by any means so valuable or interesting a one as his. However, both of them, and any more we can find, will be sent to Professor Bell, of the Natural History branch of the British Museum, to-morrow morning by the parcel post, and in the meantime are carefully consigned to a special bottle by themselves, that no rash intruder, no gormandising crab or starfish, may endanger the least of their polyps; and all faces are happier—I was going to add all appetites keener, but that is impossible—as we sit down to our well-earned luncheon on the island, where we land to picnic and stretch our legs before we resume our dredging.

But what is there in this sea-rush which makes it so interesting, even to an unscientific inquirer like myself? Because it has all the charms of an unexplored country—there are still new facts to be ascertained about it; and even in this scientific age it is perfectly evident that the last word of its history has not yet been written. There is not even any really good picture of it in any work upon natural history, whether technical or popular; even the drawings in Professor Marshall's interesting and able work on the Oban Pennatulidæ cannot be considered satisfactory by those who have had the opportunity of watching the living creature for weeks together. As it comes up in the dredge, an ordinary specimen resembles a knitting-needle, stocking-making size —if I was a lady, or it was a fish-hook, no doubt I might identify it by a number—made of a white, hard, brittle, chalky material, and covered with small fleshy pink appendages to within a short distance of both extremities. Each of these ends has been flat, as if broken off short, in every specimen except one that I have seen. That one was the small one my boy has just picked out of the net, which terminates at one end in a small bulb, a circumstance which quite justifies his exultation, and his request that when it goes to the Museum it may be described as being of his discovery. No collection in the world possesses a perfect specimen. There is only one known example—at Glasgow—which is feathered with polyps to the top; while even that one is without the bulb, which is the glory of my specimen, and which is unquestionably of very rare occurrence, although not so absolutely unique as one complete at the other extremity. In sea water the fleshy appendages expand as little flower-like polyps, united to the stalk by a semi-transparent medium, each capable of a separate existence, and to be seen under the microscope feeding healthily " with the pinnules grasping an animalcule and gently conveying it to the mouth." It is this curious mutilated condition of the ordinary virgularia—the problems it suggests, still unsolved in my opinion—and the hope of attaining the pinnacle of a collector's ambition, which makes it so interesting. Small and insignificant as it may be, the first discoverer of an absolutely perfect specimen ought to feel

> " Like some watcher of the skies
> When some new planet swims into his ken."

What, then, are the reasons given by writers upon this curious zoophyte to account for the fact that while perfect specimens are supposed to terminate in a feather at one end and a bulb at the other, like its first-cousin, the sea-pen (*Pennatula phosphorea*), it has never been found with both, and seldom with either? To put it shortly, their theory is, that it stands up with its bulb planted in the mud, and that fish invariably bite off the feathered end, while the brittle nature of the stem, and a power it apparently possesses of drawing itself back when touched or pulled, accounts for the root being almost always broken by the

OUT OF THE DEPTHS

dredge or trawl at the depth of fifteen to thirty fathoms.

Then, is it established conclusively that these creatures live planted upright in the manner suggested? I confess I was thoroughly sceptical on this point until I was referred by a passage in Marshall's book to Darwin's "Voyage of the *Beagle*," page 126 of the edition of 1889. He there describes a kind of sea-pen (*Virgularia patagonica*) which he saw at Bahia Blanca. "At low water hundreds of these zoophytes might be seen, projecting like stubble with the truncate end upwards a few inches above the surface of the muddy sand. When touched or pulled they suddenly drew themselves in with force, so as nearly or quite to disappear. By this action the highly elastic axis must be bent at the lower extremity, where it is naturally slightly curved. . . . It is always interesting to discover the foundation of the strange tales of the old voyagers; and I have no doubt but that the habits of this virgularia explain one such case. Captain Lancaster, in his voyage in 1601, narrates that on the sea sands of the island of Sombrero, in the East Indies, he 'found a twig growing up like a young tree, and on offering to pluck it up it shrinks down to the ground and sinks, unless held very hard.' On being plucked up, a 'great worm is found to be its root, and as the tree groweth in greatness, so doth the worm diminish, and as soon as the worm is turned into a tree it rooteth into the earth and so becomes great.'"

I have quoted the passage at length because it is absolutely the only direct evidence as to the upright habit of the virgularia; all the rest is conjecture, possibly well founded, but still conjecture only, derived from its shape and structure, and appearance when obtained. I, of course, accept Darwin's evidence absolutely on a point he vouches as an eye-witness, but it did not seem to me entirely to conclude the controversy as regards the British species, which is an inhabitant of deep water, and which no one has seen in its natural position. I therefore examined the collection at the British Museum in order to find out how far the Bahia species is identical with, or similar to, the British, but unfortunately it contains no example of *Virgularia patagonica*. I am bound, however, to add that the specimens of virgularia from Trinidad and Panama are sufficiently analogous in appearance to the British to justify the conclusion that their habits are likely to be similar. From the appearance of the creature in confinement, I should have considered it impossible that it could withdraw itself into the soil when touched. It is very stiff and brittle, and does not present any appearance of muscular energy, or of that peculiar elasticity which Darwin alludes to. I fully admit, however, that the balance of evidence is decidedly in favour of its occupying an upright position in the mud, and I accept that theory as probable, if not absolutely and conclusively demonstrated; but I think writers are going too far when they not merely treat this as indisputable, but use it as an argument conclusively establishing similar habits on the part of its British first-cousins, the sea-rope and the sea-pen. With regard to these two, I shall have a word to say later on, and in the case of the latter, at least, I think I can produce strong affirmative evidence tending to a contrary conclusion. Next, as to the cause of its curious mutilation. It does not appear in either of the other sorts, and yet their tops look as if they would be far more tempting to a fish than those which they are supposed to devour so greedily. Codfish and haddocks, the suspected culprits, are not common at the spot where I have obtained my specimens, and it is difficult to believe that out of the numbers discovered only one should have escaped the voracity of such enemies. No one who has studied marine zoology at all would be inclined to doubt that an incessant struggle for existence, and ceaseless slaughter goes on beneath the waves, but I hesitate to condemn the fish on the evidence produced as yet. It is, however, a curious confirmation of their guilt, as far as it goes, that of five fragments of virgularia taken by Mr. Darbishire, of Manchester, from a haddock's stomach near Scarborough, no less than three should be tops, which is certainly significant when we remember that only one specimen has ever been dredged perfect in respect of that part. On the other hand, it must be remembered that Darwin describes the specimens he saw by hundreds at Bahia as truncated.[1]

With regard to the Funiculina, or sea-rope, I will say very little, as I have only seen it once, except in a museum. It is much longer, larger, and more elastic than the other allied species; is often obtained perfect, and attains as great a length as five feet. It has a curious square

---

[1] Note on the *Virgularia mirabilis*.—Subsequently to the date (August 1890) when the above article was written, I had many better opportunities of studying the Virgularia. I dredged one large specimen with the bulb intact which may now be seen in a side case in the room at the British Museum in Cromwell Road devoted to British zoology. It is very well preserved, and will repay inspection, although it conveys no idea of the beauty of a living specimen. I no longer have any doubt that all specimens naturally exist with a bulb planted in the soft mud, as I have had the opportunity of testing the fact by experiment. I dredged a good many small specimens with the bulb intact (when two or three inches long, they are much softer and less brittle than larger specimens), and put them in a wide-mouthed pickle jar filled with sea-water, and some of the muddy sediment which comes up in the dredge with them when they are found. They soon fixed themselves upright in the mud, and throve so well in their environment that I succeeded in keeping some of them alive for two months under constant observation. When touched with a camel's-hair brush they rapidly retracted themselves into the mud in the manner described by Darwin; sometimes disappearing altogether. The calcareous stem hardens as they grow older, and becomes so brittle as to fully account for the rarity of the bulb coming up in the case of mature specimens.

calcareous stem or bone; and my boatman, a most accurate and intelligent observer, described it to me minutely before I had ever read of it or seen it in spirits. He said he had got great numbers at a place near Ballachulish, and that the schoolmaster, who was an ardent fisherman, had told him, accurately as it turned out, that wherever they were found, it was sure to be a good mark for haddocks. He described the creature as a sea-pen, about the length and thickness of the handle of an umbrella, and added that his friend the schoolmaster had ingeniously made picture frames with the white ivory-like "bones" arranged in diminishing sizes.

With regard to the sea-pen (*Pennatula phosphorea*), I can speak from considerable personal experience. There are at least two of my specimens—one dried, the other in spirits—exhibited at the British Museum, and I brought them another alive last November, which lived some days, and excited much interest before he succumbed to change of scene and diet, and the fatigues of the journey. One point, at least, he settled before his decease. Dr. Johnstone, in his "History of British Zoophytes," says in opposition to the opinion of former observers, that he does not move. "When placed in a basin or plate of sea-water, the pennatulæ are never observed to change their position." Certainly this one moved freely in the tank, as did others

I have observed, and Professor Bell called my attention to the trail he had left behind him. The sea-pen is a beautiful object, its great feather-like pinnæ expanded and waving, with all their little flower-like polyps out and on the alert, and its semi-transparent quill expanding and contracting, and its general appearance exactly resembling the feather of some curious bird. The Latin names, with their English equivalents, sea-rope, sea-pen, sea-rush, are a true boon to the unscientific naturalist, and I could wish that all other species were christened as suggestively, according to their appearance, instead of merely commemorating by their names the vanity of their first discoverers, and illustrating the difficulty of coining European surnames into tolerable Latin.

With regard to these creatures the older opinion invariably was, that they often swam about near the surface. The curious may read the various statements of earlier observers, collected to be contradicted in Johnstone's work. Bodasch, the original discoverer of the Funiculina, asserts that he saw the sea-pens swimming in a beautiful phosphorescent light in 1749, when going to Marseilles. I lighted upon a curious confirmation of this when searching the Museum for the virgularia Darwin saw at Bahia. Among the collection of sea-pens, I found what was evidently the calcareous centre of one, described in Gray's catalogue of 1870 as *Osteocella Cliftoni*. It is labelled as follows: "The backbone taken out of the marine animal in bottle marked No. I. I caught him swimming with great rapidity in shallow water.—G. Clifton." The catalogue proceeds (the bottle never reached the Museum): "It has much the appearance of being the bone or axis of a pennatula, but *they hardly swim with great rapidity.*" I am glad to say that the words in the Museum catalogue are marked with an imperative *d*, which I suppose means *dele*. Probably the corrector agrees with me that it is better to accept the testimony of an eye-witness in the first instance, making all due allowance for inaccuracy or exaggeration, having regard to the character, temperament, and previous record of the observer himself. It is hardly necessary to remind my readers of the many instances in which travellers' tales, disbelieved and discredited at home, have turned out to be true, thus turning the tables upon the uncivil and incredulous. I cannot, from personal observation, throw any light upon the question whether the sea-pen swims or not; but I think I can help to disprove its alleged erect position in the mud. In the first place, all the specimens I have yet obtained have come, not from a soft muddy bottom, but from a bank of hard sand, where they have come up entangled in the long line set for plaice or flounders, or transfixed by one of the hooks. I was not alive to all the conditions of the problem until the present year; but I can vouch that the last specimen I obtained had a hook right through the extreme tip of the bulb of the quill, which is alleged to be buried inches deep in the mud. I am not writing a scientific treatise, but my digression is not without an object. Oban, the most favoured haunt of the Pennatulidæ, is also the summer head-quarters of innumerable yachts. Many owners, it is roundly asserted, are not altogether innocent of splashing for sea trout at the mouths of the rivers, in defiance of the law, and other poaching practices; while some, alas, sink so low as to persecute and harry the beautiful, innocent, and useful sea-gulls and terns. Let them rather exert their energies in the attempt to solve such problems as I have indicated, and the many others which every day's dredging suggests. If they will only try it, they will find their reward in a new reason for visiting scenes of wonderful beauty, and in an amusement of surpassing interest. Amateur trawlers, also, and professionals, might do good service by keeping an eye to the rubbish; it fills my soul with profound melancholy to think what treasures are daily thrown away under that contemptuous designation. I may suggest experiments to managers of aquaria, especially at such stations as Rothesay, Oban, and Glasgow. There are also further points to be investigated, such as the nature, extent, and origin of the phosphorescence which is another characteristic of all the creatures, and the reason why the sea-pen is called *Pennatula phosphorea*. Is this light electrical, or due to some spontaneously inflammable substance? or is it due to special phosphorescent organs, bands of fatty substance —"cordoni luminosi," as Panceri calls them in his studies on the phosphorescence of marine animals? Lastly, as Darwin says, "What is an individual?" How suggestive is the fact that these creatures are, from one point of view, the homes of innumerable polyps, feeding independently, and even capable of separate existence; while from another they are one creature retreating into the mud, in the instance of the sea-rush, crawling and waving its feathers with one motion, in that of the sea-pen; even if its swimming rapidly, or at all, is treated as disproved! If a colony, how obedient are its subjects! if a unit, how singularly independent are its different parts!

But it is high time that we should return to our dredging, and this time we pass across nearly to the other side of the loch before we let down our net for a draught. As we row across, a seal puts up his round, shiny head within fifty yards of the boat, and after a good stare, dives down as if he did not like the looks of the party; and he only reappears after some five minutes, as a mere speck on the surface of the water. I do not even grasp at the rifle, which is in its cover at the bottom of the boat; but it was the death of a seal which, on a former occasion, enabled me to find the right place for dredging up the Serpulæ, which are so beautiful either alive as aquarium specimens, or dead as coral-like ornaments. I had finished my lunch on the island a little lower down than we are now, and was enjoying the pipe of peace, and watching the buzzards wheeling round the opposite peak, and two old ravens soaring, croaking over my head, when a seal made his appearance suddenly within fifty yards. The opportunity was too good to be lost, as I had promised a skin to a friend, and in another instant he was struggling on the surface, soon to struggle no more. He floated until the boat, hastily launched, almost touched him, but sank just as the men were reaching out the boat-hook towards him. Next morning the boatmen easily recovered his body with the small trawl-net, and with it a quantity of very large white twisted tubes, which I found on the rock where they had been thrown away. Next day saw me round at the same place with the dredge, and in the first haul, just where the seal had sunk, the net came up quite full of these Serpulæ, far larger and more beautiful than I had ever seen before in any previous years' dredging; and this place once discovered, I have never since failed to obtain similar specimens when wanted — a good illustration how curiously local are the various sea creatures. Their large red flowers protrude from every tube, the living petals surrounding a central stopper, and retreating in an instant if the shadow of anything in motion comes across them. In this hasty disappearance they are like another tube-worm, the Sabella, which makes its tube not of lime but of sand and mud, and keeps out its large striped, brownish fan unless actually touched or molested.

I must pass rapidly over the rest of our afternoon's sport. Every now and then the contents of the dredge are discoloured with a brilliant violet dye, the unfailing indication that we have captured a sea-hare. This curious mollusc carries its shell inside, and like the cuttle-fish, exudes a quantity of colouring matter when captured or disturbed. Its name seems singularly inapplicable to the round, dark, gelatinous lump which is discovered in the middle of the violet dye, but is readily understood when once the creature has been seen crawling along, sticking up its two comical long ears. Other sea-slugs are captured; the orange-coloured Doris, its back adorned with the yellow tassel which represents its lungs, and the graceful feathery Eolis. Every haul provides specimens of the Comatula, or rosy feather-star, which should be looked upon with respect as the sole British example of the oldest family of starfish on earth, the stalked Crinoids. Every time the dredge comes up there are half-a-dozen at least of these dark-red objects limply adhering to the sides, or mixed up with harder creatures to the detriment of their brittle feathers. If put into sea water they immediately expand, and present the appearance of a living crimson-lake sea-weed, with ten slender feathery fronds extended from a common centre. If you examine them more closely, you will perceive that the ten fronds are really five arms, each divided near the point of junction with the cup-shaped base, which contains the small soft body. When young, it still more nearly resembles a plant or seaweed, as it grows attached to the sand or rock by a long simple jointed stalk, and waits until it has attained a certain degree of maturity before it breaks loose from its fetters and dares the perils of existence as a freely moving and swimming creature. Its colour varies a good deal from dark to light red, with parts of its arms often nearly white, and I have caught one of quite a sandy colour. I also once captured one of a light greyish colour, with feathers so long and hairy in their appearance, and altogether so different in its characteristics from ordinary specimens, that I almost hoped it was a new species, and not merely a curious variety. Alas! it arrived at the Museum during holiday time, and was so utterly broken to pieces before it could be examined that it was impossible to identify it. I have sent up several Comatulæ in spirits; in sea water they invariably break in pieces. Some took their place in the spirit room of the Museum with many others, to illustrate the geographical distribution of the species; others went to a distinguished scientific inquirer,[1] who was making a microscopic investigation of the parasites which infest them—a proof of the fact that the dredge opens another half-explored world to the microscopic student.

Other starfish make their appearance in large numbers; numerous specimens of the common brittle sandstar, with those long, snaky arms, from which the various members of the family take their generic name of Ophiura; quantities of beautiful rosy sun-stars, with twelve to fifteen rough, bristly rays, symmetrically arranged; of all sizes, from great fellows as big as a plate, to little ones not larger than a shilling; and, more rarely, their near relation, the purple sun-star, different in colour and shape, and much smoother in its texture, with only nine to eleven rays. Eyed cribellas also come to the surface, rosy and stiff, not looking the least like live creatures and determined enemies of the oysters, whelks and

---

[1] The late Dr. Carpenter.

scallops; and next, the curious bird's-foot sea-star, like a five-sided orange fritter, the thinnest and flattest of starfish, flexible, like a piece of leather, and composed of a whitish membrane, edged with red, like the webbed foot of a duck, uniting five red rays which extend to its angles from a centre of the same colour.

I must merely roughly enumerate other objects of interest, shells of many sorts and colours, living and dead, from great clams to tiny cowries. Red and transparent ascidians of various sizes and shapes. Creeping things innumerable; galateas like tiny lobsters, and shrimps, prawns, and sand-hoppers of varied hues. But the ducks are flying in to feed, and I have had many warning hints from the most sensible member of the party that it is time we were turning home. The very last haul of the dredge provides us with three more specimens of the sea-rush, two of them so large that they cannot go into any of our bottles, and are triumphantly consigned to the large jar of sea water which is destined to replenish the foot-tubs which we have turned for the time into aquaria. One is fourteen inches and a half long, and a special tube has to be sent from London for its transport; but neither is perfect, and I plead in vain for another turn, when perhaps the black tulip the four-leaved shamrock, may yet crown our efforts.

More prudent counsels prevail, especially as my

OUT OF THE DEPTHS

own common sense admits that we shall be late enough home as it is. For once we have a fair breeze, and not too much of it, to take us out of the loch; but, although it carries us swiftly along, the sun is setting over Jura before we turn homewards in Crinan Bay. I will not endeavour to rival Black, by describing the gorgeous colouring of cloud and hill. All is subdued to a dull purple before we reach our landing-place, but although the day has been long for all, and tiring for some, the whole party are longing for another day when they may again explore the depths of "the great and wide sea, wherein are things creeping innumerable, both small and great beasts."

CHAPTER VIII

WESTERN WATERS

TIME, four in the afternoon; and the "shower peculiar to the country" has been going on since morning with more than usual persistency. Every indentation in the hillside, every gutter in the road, the very foot-paths themselves, are temporarily transformed into rivulets, swelling the burns into turbid torrents which are pouring their tribute into the river, which in its turn has begun to "wax," a fact apparent to the initiated eye from the grass, sticks, and leaves which are floating on its surface towards the bay. It is a day which would drive a Frenchman to suicide, but it does not seem to make much impression upon the stolid farmer who has already turned his hay four times, and will certainly have to do so at least once more before carrying it, but who bears his misfortunes with a resignation engendered by custom; or upon the old wife trudging slowly along the road with her petticoats rather high-kilted, and a huge umbrella over her head, and who gives vent as she passes me to the undeniable and expressive monosyllable "Saft."

My expression is different from that of the farmer or the old crone: it is not one of resignation or stolidity, but of unmistakable elation, which would seem unaccountable to the ordinary observer of the leaden sky, the sodden landscape, and the persistent downpour. But a fisherman would have no difficulty in risking a guess at the correct explanation. He would recognise a brother of the angle, and would rightly conjecture that my thoughts were of the morrow; that my heart was swelling with the hope that springs eternal in the fisherman's breast, and that I was already settling provisionally where and when I should begin the next day.

I was born an angler, and from the first day that I was big enough to handle a rod have pursued, with varied success but unwavering perseverance, every kind of fish from the stickleback to the salmon. My father still chuckles over the recollection of my first big trout, a splendid fellow of some three-quarters of a pound, who took my worm when I was fishing for roach in a little pond some quarter of a mile from the house. Hearing unearthly shrieks, he rushed up the hill on the wings of terror, scarcely hoping to be in time to save me from a watery grave, and found me executing a war-dance and war-whoops of victory over my captive—much to his wrath at the time, but to his amusement since. As the twig is bent, the tree is inclined; and I can still excite myself over any unwonted capture, although, perhaps, I do not make quite so much noise over it as when I was nine years old.

There are pages in my memory which still enshrine my greatest success, as—the big pike I caught out of a coracle in a Kentish pond, which towed my little bark against the wind; my first salmon caught in Norway in 1862; my first twenty-pounder from the Tay; and last, not least, another twenty-pound fish which I landed by myself with a trout rod and small fly, in the little Argyleshire stream I am about to describe, where such monsters are rare indeed. There are few kinds of British field-sports to which I am altogether a stranger; but, although each has its attraction, I still keep my warmest devotion for my first love.

There is no kind of sport in which one is so entirely independent of extraneous aid; there is doubtless a romance and an excitement about the pursuit of the noblest of Scotch beasts of chase, the red deer, in the solitude of the forest; but there is the decided drawback that you are usually handed over to the tender mercies of a stalker, whose commands you are implicitly bound to obey, and who may or may not condescend to give you a reason for them; and there is also the necessity for a tail of gillies and ponies. So grouse-shooting requires keepers, dogs, and ponies; and covert-shooting, and even partridge-shooting under modern conditions, need assistants and companions to be successfully carried out. It is only in France, if anywhere, that—

> "Shouldering your *rifle*, and winding your horn,
> You chase the pink partridge that chirps in the corn."

But the fishing to which I am now looking forward may be, and will be, done by myself only; and it is this which makes me love the little Add more than more famous and romantic rivers where fish run much larger, but where gillies, and probably boats as well, are absolutely necessary. I dislike the sensation of being watched; I hate well-meant advice as to flies and places; and I abhor the ejaculation "There he is!" or words to a like effect, which no gillie can restrain when a fish rises, and which produce the involuntary and premature motion of the wrist or arm which has saved the life of many a gallant salmon and trout.

Next morning the sky is clear, and half a gale of wind is blowing. There are a few ominous-looking clouds on the hills, which indicate that there will be "some showers" in the course of the day, which may be interpreted to mean heavy plumps of rain, lasting about three-quarters of an hour each, which defy an umbrella or an ordinary overcoat, and would easily reduce a Parisian or a Londoner to the condition of damp blotting-paper; but the probability is not in the least alarming to a Highland fisherman. With long wading-stockings, and a thick mackintosh, I care as little for the prospect of rain as an ironclad for old-fashioned ordnance, or a knight in mail for the pikes and arrows of an ill-armed peasantry. A glance through my glass from the window at the river, about three miles off, shows me that the water, although high, is not too much so for fishing purposes; it is two feet below the bank, at a spot below a white gate, which is my regular mark from the house, and a very short time sees me off in a dog-cart, suitably clothed and equipped, bound for the upper part of the river, the most likely place for a fish when the water is high. A waterproof in a case is slung over one shoulder, and a bag with two divisions over the other: one partition, of india-rubber, contains my lunch, knife, flask, reel, and tin box of flies and casts, and a gaff to screw into the landing handle; the other, of canvas, is intended, and, I hope, destined, to hold fish before the day is out. A folding telescope landing-net hangs from the strap of the bag, and a fourteen-feet three-jointed double-handed trout rod completes an equipment which, assuredly, would not do for the Spey or Tay. Off I drive, my hopes rising higher and higher as I get nearer and nearer to the water-side.

Hood's immortal footman, after his ascent of Mont Blanc, is anxious to describe the glacier, which he does as follows: "Arter sliping and sliding for 'ours, we come to the fust principle glazier. To give a correct noshun, let any won suppose a man in fustions, with a fraim and glass and puttey, and a dimond pensel, and it's quit the revers of that!" In like manner I must ask any one to disabuse himself of all preconceived notions of a salmon river, whether derived from books or experience, in order that he may understand the one I am about to visit. Imagine a noble stream, now pouring down in cataracts, now breaking white in rapids, and now rushing black, deep, and oily around boulders at the foot of a fall—and it is quite the reverse of that. At the upper part of its short course near its source it is, indeed, wild and rapid enough, but there it is little fished; from thence it gradually winds through an almost level plain; rock and gravel becoming rarer and rarer, the stream deader and duller, and its bends more and more circular as it approaches the sea. Looking down upon its course from the hill, it is not difficult to see what geology and history confirm; that the great peat moss through which it flows must at no very distant date, geologically speaking, have formed a part of the sea itself, and that the queer rocky hill, Dunadd, which stands out like an island in the middle, was an actual island in days gone by. There it was that Pharaoh's daughter landed in pursuit of Moses, and I have myself seen her footprints on the rock at the summit, nearly two feet long and broad in proportion—a beetle-crusher sufficiently formidable to account for the secret and precipitate flight of the Israelitish law-giver. From that point the river winds more and more through the flat, until its course resembles a double S near the point where it flows into the sea at Crinan. All the lower part is tidal, and there is a chance of getting a grilse, or a basket of sea-trout near the mouth at "first of flood," even when it is hopeless to attempt to fish the upper portion of the stream. It is necessary for success that there should be a good curl on the water, which can only be the case when there is half a gale blowing, as the banks are high above the stream and shelter it from the wind.

But to-day I am bound for the "Irishman's pool," and although the old horse rattles me along at a good pace, he appears to be crawling, so eager am I to get to work. As I pass the bend of the river at Drimvaur, and cross the bridge at Kilmichael, I can see that "she'll fish fine"; and, as I sit down and put my rod together by the pool, I can see three or four fish moving in a manner which increases my impatience. However, I am too old a hand to neglect precautions in my haste, and my cast is carefully soaked and straightened, and the joints of my rod firmly tied together before I select my flies, a small blue doctor for the tail-fly, and two very small sea-trout flies, a claret body and an orange, for droppers. Of course, droppers would not do in many salmon rivers, but in this one there are but few stones, and what there are I know well; and I have often been surprised at the luck I have had with them: the salmon taking the tiny flies when they have refused the larger.

Above me, on the opposite bank, is the wood of Kirnan, called after the farm just above, the birthplace of the poet Campbell, and the scene of the "desolate garden" he found on "revisiting Argyleshire." If his ghost were to walk there now he would not find "one rose of the wilderness left on its stalk, to show where a garden had been," or anything at all resembling the ideal landscape depicted by Millais on the subject, but substantial farm-buildings, with oats and potatoes growing up to the very door. The pool is the shape of a horse-shoe, or, rather, of a boomerang. The river runs sharply over a shallow at the top, and deepens under the opposite bank, running briskly till it comes to the turn, where a backwater is formed by a little burn running at an angle. From thence there is a deep oily narrow neck for about fifteen yards, with two rocks just projecting at the top, and then it widens, till it joins the shallow below by two channels with a point of gravel between them. I wade in at the top, for, although it is not a long cast, the fish rise right under the hazel and oak-scrub overhanging the opposite side, and the fly plays best with a rather short line. At the second cast there is a sharp tug, and a turn of the reel; but the water is too shallow just here for a real " fish." Short shrift has my victim; a nice little silvery sea-trout, of about a pound weight, with every disposition, if permitted, to frolic and splash about the pool and alarm his betters. If I gave him an inch he would take an ell; but I do not, and he is lying gasping on the bank before he has had time to be surprised at the results of greediness or curiosity. A little lower down the reflection of a white stone shows just through the water, and there I feel a conviction, amounting to certainty, that something better will come, and I am not disappointed. There is a curl and a glint of silver, and at the next cast he is fast, and shaking his head, with a slow deliberate movement, from side to side, which denotes that he is lightly hooked, and thinks that he may get rid of his incumbrance without the trouble of a run for it. While he is making up his mind I am wading out, for I like to play my fish from above them, and with a fairly long line, and also prefer *terra firma* to slippery pebbles. I am not without hopes that a little gentle persuasion may prevent him from dashing along the other side and disturbing his "neighbours," and I am not disappointed, for in a few minutes he is safe round the corner, well in hand, taking decent and respectable runs, and I take advantage of his pacific disposition to unscrew the net and substitute the gaff; laying the handle across the left arm ready for action. It sounds awkward, but, with patience and choice of the right moment, I have never experienced the least difficulty in a task which would seem to require a third hand. But the fish takes advantage of his second wind, and the reel whirs and the line sings, as he makes a determined rush for the bottom of the pool, flinging himself out of the water twice in his course, and showing the neat proportions of a handsome grilse of eight pounds weight, or thereabouts. That rush was his last serious effort, and, as his tail plays slowly on the surface of the pool, I shift the rod to my left hand, and stretch out my right, with the gaff in it, and in another moment I have slackened the line by letting out two or three turns, the rod is on the ground, and the fish is on the bank, receiving his quietus with a stone. Soon the fly is cut out, and the sport is resumed.

I am not going to weary the reader with a description of an entire day's fishing. Catching one fish, on paper, is very like catching another, although there is an infinite variety in reality. Often have I spent the greater part of the day by the Irishman's pool alone, small as it is, and I have taken out of it as many as five salmon, besides losing others. If one of my captures has been disagreeably restive, I have gone to the pool above for a short time, or I have indulged in lunch or a pipe; but it is wonderful how soon salmon, or other fish, seem to forget the misfortunes of their friends. "Call that a pool!" said a friend who was introduced to the Irishman's pool for the first time, after some experience of Tay and Tweed. "Why, it is no bigger than a washing-basin." Yet have I, *horresco referens*, seen more than a hundred salmon taken out of it with one haul of the net, when low water, and the need of removing temptation from the poachers, compelled the use of that atrocious implement. The "Irishman" is not an easy pool to net by night, but there are places where salmon get shut in, in low water, where they can, and do occasionally, fall victims to every description of implement. A sharp knife at the end of a stick, giving a quick slash at their tails; a hay-fork;

a sheep net weighed down with a ploughshare —to these and similar ignoble methods have many gallant fish succumbed from time to time. I have counted them, on one day, in a pool from which there was no possibility of exit except from above, and on the morrow have mourned over their reduced numbers, and the scars of some of the survivors. Still, poaching is not very common, and the course of the river is so open that it is easily detected.

I wonder whether I shall ever recover the gaff I lost in the "Irishman" last year? I had hooked a fish, and was playing him in bright sunshine, when suddenly, and without the slightest warning, down swept a squall from the hillside, accompanied by torrents of rain, straight in my face, so violent that it was difficult to stand and hold my rod upright. Before I had got my fish I was soaked to my wading-stockings; my mackintosh, alas! lay on the bank above me, and my fingers were numb, and my rod sending rivulets of water down my sleeves. I brought the fish within reach, and gaffed him, but the slippery landing-handle escaped from my grasp, and it bobbed up and down three or four times in the deepest part of the pool, and then sank to rise no more. The fish, however, was still on, and gained nothing except the sweets of revenge; for he was out on the bank in a minute more, receiving a peculiarly vicious tap upon the nose as a punishment for the theft of which he had been guilty.

Have I ever caught two salmon at a time? Well, never; although I have once known a fish to hook himself upon two flies, taking both with a continuation of the same rise. Of course, with sea or river trout such an adventure is too common to be worth relating, but I have only known one well-authenticated instance with salmon, and then the gillie who gaffed and landed the fish displayed a presence of mind which showed the qualities of a great general. The fish had followed one another kindly in their rushes, and were both exhausted on the surface; but the crucial question was how to get the one out who had taken the dropper without a dead pull at the line, which would break the cast or the hook between the pair of artificial Siamese twins. As the fish approached the bank, the attendant gaffed it with one hand, and, with an almost simultaneous movement of the other, cut the dropper from the cast with a sharp knife, and was rewarded to his sagacity and luck by seeing the other fish also succumb in a few moments more. If such attendants were common, I might be fempted to forswear my solitary habits.

The rustic who waits for the river to flow down has passed into a proverb, but those who would catch fish in the Add must not be ashamed of emulating his example. The deep-cut sheep-drains bring down the showers from the hills so fast, that I have known it too high to fish one day, and too low for much chance the next. Many a time have I gone out in a downpour, when it showed signs of clearing, and waited by the bank, watching my miniature cairn of stones put up just below high-water mark, and waiting till the appearance of its top above the surface proved that the water had begun to fall, and goodly has sometimes been the reward I have reaped for my faith and perseverance. As for gales, they are disagreeable to face in an open plain, but it is hardly possible for the wind to blow too hard for success, and I have had excellent sport when the waves were literally breaking on the pools, and it was only possible to keep the fly in the water by lowering the top of the rod till it touched the surface. In all the lower part of the river there is little or no rock, and the stream gradually hollows out the banks until the sides fall in, changing pools into shallows, and sometimes altering the whole course of the river. It is no use here to rely upon tradition alone. The fisherman must judge himself, to a great extent, where it is worth while to cast a fly; and sometimes must be wary in approaching the edges of the stream. I remember one day, when I was playing a salmon, and it was sulking in a deep hole just below me, I suddenly tumbled on the top of him, with about a ton of earth, which had given way under my weight. I managed to keep hold of the rod, but by the time I had regained my footing in the water, and had got the point upright again, he was seventy yards above me, and had taken advantage of the slack line to get round a clod or boulder and make his escape. I can confidently recommend a labourer's allotment, and a man upon it, thrown into the water, as a means of moving a sulking fish, but the remedy is a little violent.

Much has been written by humanitarian sentimentalists on the cruelty of sport in general and fishing in particular; but I comfort myself in the belief that the sense of feeling in fishes cannot be acute. I have caught a sea-trout with a fly, still bleeding from the fresh mark of a heron's bill, which had transfixed it through the middle of its body; and it would be easy to multiply instances of insensibility to pain. So, too, fish seem to have extraordinary power of recovering from the most severe injuries. I have taken a salmon in the Tay with a scar on his side nearly the size and depth of an ordinary tea-cup, quite healed, and covered over with scales, evidently the work of a seal in the estuary, and from the growth of the fish it must have been done not long before, at all events during the same year and season.

But it is time to draw these rambling remarks to a conclusion. If it were always

> "Truth the poet sings,
> That a sorrow's crown of sorrow is remembering happier things,"

then, indeed, to recall the river, and the northern breezes, in a September session in London, with the thermometer at 85°, and the echoes of voices condemned by the long-suffering Speaker for tedious iteration and irrelevancy still ringing in one's ears, would be a penance too severe. But for me, my thoughts recall the pleasures of hope as well as those of memory. In fancy I am already plodding along the well-known banks, the whistle of the curlew and the plover sounding in my ears. The snipe startle me as they rise under my feet; the great herons flap lazily away as I turn a corner just above them; the merganser brings its numerous family up the stream between the high banks into the very pool I am fishing, and then the whole troop, suddenly "spying strangers," dive about and separate, disturbing my sport for the time, but giving me a pleasure quite as great in watching them. The grouse crow upon the oat-stubbles beside me, or the old black-cocks dash over my head in flocks of ten or fourteen. Perhaps there may be a hen harrier beating the moss beside me, with the regularity of a pointer, or a merlin hawking some lark or pipit; and whether the fish rise, as they do sometimes, or whether they decline, as they do even more often, I shall return peaceful and contented to a well-earned dinner, and a sleep unbroken by dreams of political warfare.

CHAPTER IX

NIL DESPERANDUM

WHAT fisherman will ever forget the long drought of the autumn of 1894? While yachtsmen, ladies, farmers, labourers, and hotel-keepers were blessing the unwonted and continuous sunshine which prevailed from August 18 to October 25, one universal cry of lamentation and anguish poured from the lips of unfortunates by the banks of every Highland stream, from Thurso to Tweed, as they tapped the aneroids which declined to fall, and watched in vain—morning and night—for the clouds that never came. It was rumoured —I do not know with what truth—that one angler, who rented the best stretch of a celebrated river, at a total cost of little less than £1000 for the season, only secured one small grilse in over ten weeks; and this was but an exaggerated sample of the meagre nature of the harvest reaped by hundreds. Yet it was at the very close of this period, when springs were dry which had never "given out" during the memory of the oldest inhabitant, and when it was almost impossible in the wettest district of

Ross-shire to find enough water to perform the necessary ablutions after the death of a stag, that the little river where I have fished for over a quarter of a century gave me the best week's sport I have ever experienced.

On October 13, the morning broke dull, misty, and still, with a little drizzle falling. We had intended to take a walk after wild grouse, but the day was not inviting, and after waiting till about eleven o'clock in the hope of its clearing, I took my trout rod and strolled off to the river —rather jeered at by my host; but, although I had not much hope of sport, I knew that I could amuse myself for an hour or two watching the stream, which I had not seen for more than a year. My mackintosh I left at home—a piece of rashness I should not have been guilty of many years ago. A small bag contained my lunch, reel and fly-book, and a net and gaff to screw into my landing-handle, while its outer partition seemed likely to be more than large enough for anything I might have to bring home. A light, but fairly stiff, split cane trout rod completed my equipment, and three-quarters of an hour later I was crossing the foot-bridge over the river; and as I looked upon and through the glassy surface, and counted the stones below, I felt that there was only one place which I could try with any chance of success. Most of the lower water is guarded by deep banks, but there is a long horseshoe-shaped pool, about a mile from the mouth, with a low, shelving gravel bank on opposite sides at each turn, some part of which is sure to catch every breeze that blows. No time was to be lost, as next day was full moon, and the tide would be in by half-past one o'clock at the latest; so a very few more minutes saw me at the head of the pool with my rod put together, and two small sea-trout flies—a blue doctor and a nondescript with black body and silver twist on a medium loch-trout cast.

There was only a very slight ripple on the water, but at about the third cast something large turned at the fly, and I caught a glimpse of a silvery side as the fish returned to its fastness at the bottom. A short pause, then another cast, and the salmon rose again in the same place—a third—and I was fast in the first fish of the year, which dashed off across the pool almost as much surprised as I was. I treated him with becoming deference, waited till he sulked a minute before I screwed the gaff into the handle, and in a short time administered the *coup de grâce* to a handsome grilse weighing 7 lb. I will not enter into a detailed account of the events of the next two hours, but before the tide came in I had risen a number of fish, and killed two more grilse of 6 lb. each, besides an ugly, large, red kipper, weighing

9½ lb. By the time these were landed the tide had begun to run strongly upwards, bringing with it a nice lot of fresh sea-trout, of which I secured six in the next twenty minutes.

Fishing was then over for the day, as it is only at "first of flood" that even sea-trout rise for a short time, while salmon stop rising as soon as the gravel begins to be flooded off the shoals. So I collected the fish and hid them in a tuft of rushes, and after luncheon and a pipe, walked home, calling at the keeper's on the way to tell him to send for the fish, which I did not care to carry back myself.

Tuesday found me again in the same place, and although I could only fish for a short time before the tide came in, I got two salmon weighing 18 lb. between them, and lost another I had nearly landed, on a bit of wire fence which had at some time been washed in, and which I could plainly see in the deep part of the water bending as the fish struggled before the final catastrophe. The only other adventure of the day was that a second fish took the tail fly after I had nearly landed one on the dropper, and pulled his predecessor off in his eager struggle to escape, falling a victim himself to his philanthropic efforts.

Three times during that eventful week did I have two salmon on at a time, but I never succeeded in landing both of them, though once, at least, I was sufficiently near it to hope against hope for success. The next day, in the same water, fishing till four o'clock (the tide was now growing more obliging), I beat all previous records. I had become alive to the fact that the pools were swarming with fish, and that they were as greedy as they were numerous: so I suggested in the morning that a gillie should come down to the pool after luncheon on the chance of finding something to carry up. I shall never forget Duncan's face of surprise when he came down to where I was fishing, and found the banks of the long pool fairly strewn with fish. He walked off to a neighbouring cottage for a sack, and a little later staggered to the road bearing it on his back laden with ten fish, the largest $17\frac{1}{2}$ lb., the smallest $4\frac{1}{2}$ lb., and then waited till he could deposit his burden in a friendly peat cart homeward bound.

The next day the same pool yielded seven salmon, and Friday was the only blank day I had. Blue sky, white frost, brilliant sunshine, and absolute calm were too much for even the greedy and unsophisticated denizens of the pool, and during a great part of the day I sat on the bank, chatting to the keeper, who joined me for a short time on his rounds, and told me that he had counted over ninety fish in one pool higher up, waiting to take advantage of any change of sky or atmosphere. Even upon this hopeless day many fish followed the fly, and one or two were on for a few seconds; but the odds were too great, and when Duncan appeared with his sack, all ready this time, he had to carry it away empty. Fools the fish might be, but they were not such fools as to attach themselves to gut so glaringly visible.

Such a day—so still and bright, with a peculiar scorching feeling about the sun, is often a "weather breeder," as they call it on the West Coast, and I was not surprised the next morning to see a cloudy sky, and tree tops bent by half a gale of wind. The long spell of fine weather was evidently coming to an end, but in the meantime I had one really first-rate fishing day before me, and it was with high hopes that I started for the river, although I hardly thought it possible that I could beat my previous "record" of ten salmon a day. Hitherto I had dispensed with an attendant, and gaffed and landed all the fish myself, but to-day I told Duncan to follow as soon as our sandwiches were ready, and by 10.30 I had reached the river-side. This time I did not cross the foot-bridge, as I had a fancy to try the pool where the keeper had seen so many fish the day before, and there was abundance of wind—enough to affect even the most sheltered casts. The event proved that I was right, as my fly had hardly touched the water before I was into a fish which I had some difficulty in landing, as there was a lot of weed close to the bank on my side of the river; still, before the gillie had arrived I had disposed of a nice little grilse of 6 lb., and removed my dropper, fully convinced that it was not a safe place in which to continue to fish with two flies.

A remarkable experience followed. The whole pool, as far as it was fishable, was not more than fifty yards long, and about thirty-five yards wide—yet I never left it till I went home at five o'clock in the evening. So freely did the fish rise, that I did not like to leave off even for lunch, but ate my sandwiches standing up. There were one or two spots which I never passed without a rise, and nothing seemed to frighten the fish, which absolutely declined to take any warning by the struggles of their hooked companions. They seemed quite mad for the fly, and although I was broken once or twice by my gillie gaffing the line in his excitement, and some time was wasted by my experimenting vainly with a somewhat larger fly which the fish followed but would not touch, I had caught twelve fish, the largest 9 lb. and the smallest $5\frac{1}{2}$ lb., before my sport was over for the day. Even then, I believe, I might have added to the number had I persevered, but it was beginning to get dark, and I had fished the water twice over without a taking rise, so I took my departure, and thus ended this memorable week.

The totals and weights as recorded in my rough diary ran as follows :—

	Lbs.
13th, four salmon	7, 6, 9½, 6. Six trout.
16th, two ,,	9½, 8¾.
17th, ten ,,	17½, 11, 9½, 7½, 7, 7, 7, 6, 6, 4½.
18th, seven ,,	8, 10, 5¼, 6, 6, 5, 8.
20th, twelve ,,	6, 7½, 7½, 5½, 7¾, 7, 9, 6½, 7, 6, 6, 7½.

Total, thirty-five.

All these fish were caught with a 10½-feet single-handed trout rod and small sea-trout flies of not more than three varieties.

One of my sons suggested to me that I should do well not to publish those experiences if I wished to maintain my character for honesty and truthfulness. Reverence is not the distinguishing characteristic of the rising generation; but as I can call witnesses both to character and to the facts, I am content to run the risk; especially as I think my experiences may be of use to others. My success was, no doubt, largely due to circumstances wholly exceptional—and no one could have anticipated or need expect to repeat it in the same place under normal conditions. The largest number of fish I ever caught in any one year in the same river was forty-nine, the largest number in a day seven, and those results were obtained during three months' fishing with the river frequently in perfect order; so to catch thirty-five in a week, in a very small length of water, after a long drought, must be considered phenomenal, and must be ascribed partly to the enormous quantity of fish collected in the tidal part of the stream, beyond which it was impossible for them to run; and partly to some climatic influence which I can neither understand nor explain. I am an old fisherman with a tolerably varied experience, and the more I fish the less inclined I feel to lay down the law dogmatically on the habits and caprices of that most capricious of fish—the salmon. If I have sometimes met with unexpected success, I have much more often returned with an empty basket, when all conditions seemed to point to a record day; but fishing would lose its greatest charm if it lost its uncertainty — and "scent" itself is not more uncertain.

The moral I draw is that, given the necessary combination of fish and water, however low and bright the latter may be, if you fish fine enough, and use small enough flies, you need not despair. I would also add my own belief that it is a common error of fishermen to use flies unnecessarily large. With regard to rod and tackle, I am well aware that there are not many rivers where it would be safe and easy to catch salmon with a small single-handed rod, yet where I was fishing I believe that I exercised a wise discretion in my choice of a short light rod, considering the day, the water, and the period of the year. It was quite easy to keep as much strain upon the fish as my light tackle would safely bear; and the longer your rod the more difficult it is to gaff your own salmon. The pools were small and low, and the fish hardly ever attempted to leave them; and as I said before, it was easy to follow them along the banks, and unnecessary and inexpedient to let them have a great deal of line out. Of course it must also be remembered that the fish were autumn fish—in fair condition for the time of year; but not to compare with spring salmon. Another advantage of a light rod is that you can strike quick and sharply; and although I agree with those who hold that it is often a mistake to strike salmon in rough water, this rule does not apply to lochs or still, sluggish streams where it is absolutely essential that eye and hand should be quick, and act together.

CHAPTER X

A DAY WITH THE GRILSE

IT is one of the wettest mornings of this very wet autumn of the year of grace 1890. The keeper has reported in the gun-room, on being asked whether it was any good to go out on the hill, that "the dry land was over your boots," and that the birds would be quite unapproachable. Still, the glass is rising at last, and although the water has been too high to begin with yesterday and the day before, and has committed on each day the unpardonable sin of rising and flooding us out when fishing, I determine to go again to the river for two reasons: (1) the day is wholly unsuitable for any other sport or amusement; (2) I know that there are fish in the river, and this heavy flood, just as the nets are off at the mouth, with a spring-tide at its highest, must have brought in others. Besides, it has rained so much that it surely cannot rain any more; the stock must be exhausted; and lastly, if other reasons are wanting, a true fisherman requires a great deal to keep him at home. After all, the rain that fell last night can have been nothing but a mist, although it splashed round the house like a shower-bath—or, at least, it must have been less on the hills at the sources of the Add—so the dog-cart is duly ordered to be at the door at 10.30. My wife, after vainly expostulating, suggests that I should put on a pair of shooting-boots instead of waders, so that "if I should have a gleam of sanity I can walk home. Surely, at any rate, I will not take the child with me?" But, the child, an embryo schoolboy of nine, and myself, being of a different opinion, the majority of voices carry the day; and at the hour fixed for starting we both mount the dog-cart in high glee, fully persuaded that, although the rain is still falling, it really is the clearing shower which has been prophesied for the last six weeks and has arrived at last.

Faith is rewarded this time. Before we have got to the lodge the clouds are rising over Jura, and very rapidly the whole glorious panorama opens upon our view. As the mist disperses the wind freshens, and the sun actually shows signs of vitality after his long sulks. There go eight ravens over our heads, winging their way from the shores of Loch Awe to the distant islands. They may croak away; we have too firm a belief in our luck to be turned from our purpose by their dissonant voices; besides, we are used to them—it seldom happens that a day passes without our seeing or hearing several. They may be trapped upon the mainland; but there are plenty of rocky islands seldom visited where they can breed in peace. I like them better than the jackdaws, which increase and multiply in the same places and for the same reason. The one reminds me of a mastiff; the other of a mischievous yapping cur. I am tolerant of what keepers call vermin, and would never willingly permit the slaughter of a peregrine or an eagle, although I know they take toll both in moor and forest; but jackdaws and rats are my abhorrence, and any method of destroying them, *per fas* or *nefas*, has my hearty acquiescence and good-will. The eagles, alas! seldom if ever pay us a visit; but the peregrine is often with us. Only three days ago, as I was fishing the Irishman's pool, higher up the river, I was startled by the cry of a curlew evidently in distress; and immediately afterwards the bird itself settled on the stones not ten yards off, and, as I had conjectured, the cause of its terror immediately followed in the shape of a splendid hen falcon which swooped close past my head, and, seeing me, soared off with a startled flight, and was soon lost to sight over the neighbouring hill. It was ten minutes and more before the curlew would leave my society, doubtless fearing that its enemy was waiting for it not far off.

But the dog-cart has pulled up at Dunadd Bridge, and it is time that I should get out and put my rod together. As I look at the heavy stream pouring over the rocks above, and through the arches of the bridge, I mentally admit that there is no great hurry about it. My regular marks are covered, and the water is indubitably too high; but it is clear and falling. We can see by the sticks and rubbish left on the bank that it has been higher by three feet during the night, and there is even now hope of a fish in the shallows at the heads and tails of the deep pools; while later, if the day holds up, the water should arrive at a height which will fish well. Why should I despair? My little terrier Punch sets me a lesson of perseverance by dashing off at once after the same rabbit which he always hunts at this place with as much apparent assurance of success as if he had never failed before, and in a minute is digging again at the same old hole into which his enemy has frisked as usual, with a saucy jerk of his tail, as if he enjoyed the joke. Alfred, too, is evidently sanguine, and eager that I should begin, as he has already screwed the landing-net on to the handle; so I sit down, and take out the joints of my rod, a light fourteen-feet greenheart double-handed trout-rod, tie them carefully together, and pass the line through the rings. Next I try each joint of the casting-line, and select the largest blue doctor I can find in my book for a tail-fly, and a dropper of attractive appearance, a black dog, rather larger than I usually fish

A DAY WITH THE GRILSE

with on this water. The fish here prefer a small fly; but for the present, in this high flood, the great point is to let them have something they can see to attract their attention.

Poor discontented fishermen! we are never satisfied. One day we are sighing for more water, the next we are grumbling because we have too much. "Depend upon it," said the present Lord Brampton (then only Mr. Hawkins, Q.C.), when acting at the bar for two moneylenders in a scrape, "your best chance is to tell the truth." "That's what I tell my son," answered the eldest of them; "but I'm afraid he will tell too much truth." Water, like truth, is an excellent thing in moderation; but whatever may be said of the latter, you may certainly have too much of the former. The provoking thing, too, is that you may have too much one day and not enough on the next. A short Highland river, not running out of a loch, with every hill around it drained with deep sheep-drains, rises and falls almost as fast as a speculative Stock Exchange security. However, there is nothing for it but to begin, and I deposit my spare joints and my bag almost opposite a rock just showing through the breaking water, and begin to fish the lowest of the three stretches which make up the long pool of Dunadd.

This is a monotonous pool to fish; but too prolific to be neglected. It is rather difficult to manage with a small rod, because the stream is for the most part sluggish, and requires a strong wind to make it properly fishable, which, when it touches the water properly, always blows up stream. Therefore, to make the fly hang right, it is not sufficient to cast straight across. You should throw a long line across and down stream, and work the fly with the point of the rod close to the water; and this must be done often, as the line in such a position will not work long at a time. It is tiresome and monotonous at the best of times, because one part of it is so like another; but to-day, when it is too high, it is doubly tedious, because I have not that faith in the result which encourages me to persevere, and I only flog on mechanically, in order to give plenty of time for the higher pools to run down. This occupies an hour and a half, during which time nothing makes an offer at the fly except a small parr, which endeavours to hang itself on a hook nearly as big as itself; so it is with a sigh of relief that I shoulder my bag, and with my young companion make my way through a small swampy hazelwood to the next pool up the river, which is known as "Boy's" pool, in allusion, I believe, to some legendary boy, who is supposed to have met his death there.

This is a pool which, although it always holds fish, is not usually very productive. The stream

Plenty of time.

A DAY WITH THE GRILSE

runs strong at the neck, but the pool immediately after broadens into a round hole, very deep for the most part, out of which two streams run round a sort of gravelly island. This double exit causes a kind of eddy and backwater, and except at the very neck, it is impossible to keep the line straight and make the fly hang naturally. However, I again deposit my baggage, and at the second cast a heavy boil breaks the surface of the water, the line tightens and the reel whirs. Hurrah! I am into my first fish.

I shout to Alfred, who is slowly making his way up the bank, slightly bored at the proceedings so far; and the whole scene changes in an instant. Up he runs, with excitement and delight depicted on his face, just as the salmon makes a furious rush up stream, and then a jump which nearly lands him on the opposite bank. Then comes a lull while the fish sulks for a minute in the deep water in the centre of the pool, and I can assure my little attendant, who is nervously and excitedly screwing the landing-net off and the gaff on, that he has plenty of time. He has been out with me before; but it was only yesterday that he was first allowed to use the gaff, and very well he did it, landing a seven-pound fish at the first attempt. Off goes the salmon again, and after another two turns of the reel, shows himself on the surface—a good fish for this water. I generally minimise the size of my fish, but I calculate his weight at between eight and nine pounds. As he shows, Alfred dashes to the side and madly dances after him in his rushes, heedless of my shouts that, if he will keep quiet, I will bring the salmon up to him; but it is not to be this time. The fish dashes out of the pool into the stream below, and, without the least preliminary warning, the rod straightens. The hold has given way! A breathless gasp from each of us, and the tears almost rise into my small boy's eyes; but when he sees the disgust expressed upon my countenance—which, in self-defence, I must assert to be more for his sake than my own—he remembers his first duty as consoler, and, fumbling in his pocket for some propitiatory offering, says, " Never mind, father; take a nut."

Solvuntur risu tabulæ. The consolation has come, although perhaps it is not the half-ripe nut that has done it; and, hoping for better luck next time, we move on to the Stance pool, where the stream sweeps round a bend of the river near the road, ending in a wide stretch, with deep water under the opposite bank. Halfway down a small sea-trout takes the dropper and speedily finds his way into the landing-net; and just a few yards before the end, there is another swirl in the water, and the line is tight and the reel again in motion. But it is only for a few seconds. There is something in the feel

A DAY WITH THE GRILSE

of the "hold" that tells me instinctively that the fish is but lightly hooked, and I shake my head at the little gillie, who is already beginning to prepare for action, just before the line comes back slack once more—to my disappointment, but not this time to my surprise. It is rather annoying to have had two fish on and lost them both; but I am not disheartened, as the water is improving every minute, and every one that has risen has taken hold after a fashion. We shall doubtless do better presently.

A walk of a couple of hundred yards brings us to an anonymous pool at the next bend, which is quite as well worthy of attention as many that have high-sounding names. This is a river in which it will not do to rely on tradition and reputation. The banks are undermined and fall in, and tons of gravel are washed down by every spate, so that what is a deep pool one year may become a mere run or shallow the next; therefore, only those places that have some permanent natural features, such as a bridge or a rock, or those that have been the scene of some accident or event, acquire and retain the honour of a name. I can remember catching fish in this pool twenty years ago, and then until last year it was hardly worth fishing; but the opposite side was faced with stone in 1888 to prevent further damage to the bank and the adjoining fields, and it has since become a very good place for fish, with a stream at the top ending in a deep round pool at the bottom. There is an iron railing and a ditch to get over to take me to the gravelly bank at the top, and, as it is lunch-time, I choose a sheltered spot under the bank at the bottom, where I leave my boy to unpack and begin his meal, while I go up and fish the stream over for the first time; but he has not got beyond the stage of taking out the paper parcels and untying the strings when there is another whir of the reel, and a nice little fish is dashing down stream attached (firmly, I hope, this time) to the tail-fly, which bears the seductive name of "the Captain." Cake, egg-sandwiches, and cold grouse are flung down at the first sound of the reel, and Alfred comes tearing up with Punch at his heels. The fish runs well, and is soon sufficiently exhausted to bring up to the gaff; but this time the landing is the most serious matter of difficulty. I have said that my boy gaffed his first salmon yesterday, and did it well; but then he had not been worked into a state of excitement by seeing two fish lost. His first attempt is too slow, and with the second he gaffs the casting-line, when if the fish had not been thoroughly exhausted, he would have bidden us farewell; but there is luck in odd numbers, and at the third try the point goes home, and a nice little grilse is deposited on the stones. He is soon weighed

A DAY WITH THE GRILSE 173

and put into the bag. He is only five pounds; but a fish is a fish, and we need no longer fear going home with " a blank day."

Lunch is soon over, and, when two more flies have been tried on the same stream without another offer, we begin to retrace our steps down stream. Something, either a large trout or a small "fish," moved at the fly, just below the place where we had luncheon, and again after a rest and a change of fly; but, whatever he was, he did not mean business, and equally resisted the attractions of a claret-body, a small Jock Scott, and a Captain. However, I got two small trout before I am back to the Stance pool, and give them but a short shrift, as it will be about as much as I can do to finish my water by the time the dog-cart is ordered to meet us at the bridge.

Here fortune is again favourable, for a very pretty fish of a little over six pounds takes the fly under water in the deepest part, plays kindly, and comes to the gaff soon. The only difficulty this time is caused by the ill-directed zeal of my terrier Punch, who appears to have given up rabbit-hunting for the moment, and, erroneously thinking that he can help me, dashes at the fish every time I bring him near the gaff, sending him flying to the other side of the pool, and sadly disconcerting my attendant, who, however, does his duty nobly, and in spite of the disturbing element, has the salmon out on the bank the first time he gets a fair chance, and deposits him in the bag beside his predecessor, looking like a bar of silver—so bright that he cannot have left the sea many hours.

Another fish, about the same size, rises, and falls to rise no more, in the very next stream, just where the bank has been made up with some piles, and then the luck changes again. The height of the water is still improving, the breeze keeps up well, and the sky is all a fisherman could desire; but—the fish have left off rising. I change my flies half-a-dozen times, trying varieties of size and colour; but neither the Boy's pool nor the stream below, nor any part of the long pool by Dunadd, produces a single rise; and when I see the dog-cart turning the corner towards the bridge, I feel no inclination to keep the rod on the lower water waiting, but take it down at once; and soon we are "all on board," and I am lighting a meditative pipe, my little boy volubly recounting to the groom the adventures of the day, while Punch, curled up upon the bag under the seat, dreams of the rabbits he could not catch, and of the well-earned meal which awaits him on his return.

So ends an enjoyable day; and if the more fortunate captors of monsters in Canada, Norway, the Tay, the Tweed, laugh at my poor little spoils, I can at least remind them that I am able to use

A DAY WITH THE GRILSE

the lightest of tackle, and can do without boat, gillie, and many of the other accessories indispensable on their grand rivers. I have myself been among the twenty-pounders, and can conscientiously say that with treble gut and an eighteen-feet rod I have found them just as easy to catch as their smaller relations in the Add.

CHAPTER XI

LOCH-NA-LARICH

HARDLY a ripple ruffles the surface of beautiful Loch Sween, and the sun shines brilliantly from a blue unclouded sky. What breeze there is comes fitfully from the north-east, and a light haze blots out the familiar view of the Pap of Jura. The gulls float lazily round; one or two terns drop screaming down upon the small fry, and everything looks delightful except to the eye of a fisherman. But it is not a day for one to stop at home who has only just arrived from London on a short holiday, and the only question for decision is to which of the hill lochs I shall turn my steps. Loch Choilliber holds the largest trout, but it is proverbial that the best chance of sport in its deep waters is "a regular downright beast of a day," and it is so sheltered by wood and brae that it requires half a gale to produce a good curl upon its bays and inlets. So the pounders may have a rest to-day, and I determine to content myself with the nearer and more exposed waters of Loch-na-Larich. If I get no sport there a short half-hour's stroll will bring me home again; but although I advance that fact as one of the reasons for my choice, my host laughingly shakes his head, for he knows that it is not at all likely that I shall be back much before dinner-time. However, he wishes me good luck, and I am soon strolling through the wood and up the brae, accompanied by my black spaniel Ben, and by a lad carrying my luncheon, rod, and impedimenta. My mackintosh for once I determine to leave at home.

Travellers who have been in the Holy Land describe the Sea of Galilee as being of the shape of a harp, and the same simile will give a good idea of the little mountain tarn which breaks upon my view in a cup of the hills below Cruach Lussa. There is no bloom yet upon the heather which clothes the moors around it, as it is early June, but the young bracken is shooting up through last year's withered fronds; and the small birch trees which fringe the opposite side of the little bay at the near end are brilliant with their early green. Great kingcups shine like stars among the stones at the side, and the sandpipers busily flit from rock to rock, while the air is musical with their voices, and the louder bubbling breeding-season note of the curlew which hovers over the opposite brae. Two or three mallards fly away as we approach, and a matronly duck leads a numerous brood of some eleven tiny balls of down into the reeds at the far end for shelter. The boat is moored to a small pier below me, padlocked to a chain and rope, and I sit down and put my rod together, while my attendant unfastens the padlock and prepares to get all ready for a start.

And now occurs the first misfortune of the day. The gillie has duly unfastened the padlock, but the chain is broken, and at the first pull it comes away in his hands, leaving the boat still floating out of reach. I ask him what is to be done, and he replies that he must wade for it; and after I have vainly endeavoured to move it by throwing my light line across it, we determine that wading is the only plan likely to succeed. He is for going in at once, accoutred as he is, but I impress upon him that there is no hurry, and he so far indulges my weakness as to consent to take off his shoes and stockings. This does not, however, prevent his getting wet, for the water is not merely well over his knickerbockers, but nearly up to his shoulders, before he is able to reach the boat with a long stick. While he is baling, I see a rise a little to the left, just within reach of the shore, and as I drop my fly with a longish line into the circle, a little fellow rises boldly and takes the dropper, although there is no ripple on the water. I haul him out, pulling and struggling manfully considering his size, and, as I land him, find that there is a second one attached to the tail fly, and that I have caught two with my first cast. They are not so long as my hand, but I do not put them back again, for there are really too many fish in the loch, and it would be a good thing to reduce the stock. Besides, they are excellent for breakfast, and, if I am too particular about size, it is quite probable that there may not be enough for a fry. The ordinary run of fish in this loch is about three to the pound, and one is lucky if one gets one of over a pound in a good day's fishing.

And now commences the familiar but unsatisfactory process of hunting the breeze. We gaze round the loch, and make up our minds that the best chance will be in the little bay under the birches, where there appears to be a tiny ripple. As soon as we arrive there, it has entirely disappeared, and seems to have turned its attention to the very spot we have just left. It is not hard work either for rower or fisherman, and the former just holds the boat within reach of shore, while I keep dropping my three flies as lightly as possible a few yards from the rocks, and am occasionally rewarded with a shy rise, and get a few fish, some of them of quite a decent size. What determined fighters they are! They bend my light rod, and even run out a little line. If the lazy South-Country giants of the Test or Mimram had half their energy and strength, few indeed in those weedy streams would succumb to the tiny hooks and gossamer gut necessary for effecting their capture at any time but the mayfly season. I see a few alders on the water, and am most successful with an imitation of that fly, dressed pretty large and sunk rather deep. In spite of the weather, I nearly always get an offer from any fish I see rise within reach and manage to put my fly over; but although I strike very quickly, I do not succeed in touching one in three, as they see too much, and turn before they actually touch the fly. One little fish of about a quarter of a pound is hooked foul, near the ventral fin, and makes for the weeds near the bottom so stubbornly that, until I see where he is hooked, I try to persuade myself that I have at last got hold of a monster of the deep. The most productive spot is the end near the reeds, where a line of waterlily leaves are just showing. There I get one fish of nearly three-quarters of a pound, beautifully shaped and marked, which really makes a determined struggle for liberty, actually reaching the weeds and for a moment attaching the dropper to one of them, which, fortunately, is not sufficiently firm to break the casting-line.

And now for a few moments a change comes over the scene. Hitherto there has been nothing but the lightest possible ripple, and often not even that; but now a sudden blast beats down from the hills, and the light boat is flying down the loch almost too rapidly for fishing, and, in spite of the utmost exertions of the man at the oars, the boat is down over the flies almost as soon as they touch the water. Two or three fish move at the fly in the course of the drift, but none of them are hooked, as it is really impossible to keep the line properly straight and strike in a workmanlike manner. It is but an easterly squall, and falls as rapidly as it rises; and, when a toiling and laborious pull up-wind has got us nearly back to the far end of the loch, all is calm once more, and rock, hill, and reed are reflected double in the glassy surface.

The basket at the end of the day contains only thirteen trout, and although there are one or two big ones, the average weight of the whole cannot be more than a quarter of a pound—a bad day both in number and size. At this time of the year I ought to be sure of at least a couple of dozen in an afternoon of about three to the pound. I have not changed my flies much, as the rising fish have seemed contented with what was offered them—a teal and green, a zulu and an alder. My cast was a very fine one, and when for a short time I tried burn-trout flies of the smallest size on drawn gut, I did not meet with sufficient success to encourage me to persist in the experiment. I also condescended to a minnow for a short time while I enjoyed my after-luncheon pipe, but not a touch rewarded the poaching expedient. Altogether the pleasure of the day consisted rather in the delicious air, the beautiful landscape, and the life and music around me, than in the moderate sport enjoyed. All day the birds have been busy and noisy, and I have noted fourteen varieties—herring-gull, kittiwake, heron, curlew, lapwing, sandpiper, duck, coot, moorhen, blackcock, grouse, rook, jackdaw, and cuckoo, without counting the smaller birds, such as swallows, martins, pipits, and warbler, the latter of which I find it difficult to identify with certainty at any distance.

I do not, of course, record the above day's sport as a typical or satisfactory sample of the pleasures of loch-fishing. I have had many days in various spots where the basket has been heavy at the end of the day, and fish up to two pounds, with an occasional monster even larger, have rewarded my exertions. But just as marmalade has been described as "an excellent substitute for butter at breakfast," so to my mind fishing in a loch from a boat is only a substitute for the real thing, and except for a change occasionally, I would rather have indifferent sport in a river or burn than fish the finest loch in the Highlands. I am far from saying that there is no skill in loch-fishing, or that knowledge of the locality, depth of water, and favourite haunts of big fish is not highly advantageous; but a few general rules, such as to prefer places where the water is only moderately deep, and be particularly attentive round sunken rocks, under overhanging boughs, near islands, or by patches of weeds, waterlilies, or reeds, will generally enable a stranger to a loch to make a good show at the end of the day if he understands the ordinary craft of the angler. Casting is never very difficult, as you drift along with the wind, and the temptation to a good fisherman to throw an unnecessarily long line is a stumbling-block and snare, except on the rare occasions when it enables him to cast over some rather distant fish he may have seen rise. To my mind, the most difficult thing in loch-fishing is to avoid entangling your line with that of some less expert brother angler who is casting from the same boat, and is erratic in his notions of time. A quick hand at the strike and unremitting observation and patience are of course essential for success. More skill is required in fishing from the shore or wading when a loch is thickly wooded, or the banks are approachable only from a few spots; but there are very few Scotch lochs where wading or bank-fishing give satisfactory results. Usually either the water deepens too rapidly, or reed beds or marshy deposit prevent your approaching the most likely spots.

This surely cannot be compared for sport to a ramble along some beautiful Highland stream, where the practised eye takes in the possibilities of every part of each successive reach or run. "Chuck-and-chance-it fishing"! is the carping comment of the accomplished dry-fly trout-stalker of the south, to whose superior skill and mastery of the craft I bow with an awe and admiration entirely true and unfeigned. But although I may not have marked the three-pounder sucking down olive duns among the cresses, or seen the feeding fish lying near the surface, I must demur to the cynical description of my proceedings. Chuck I do, and chance it I must, to a certain extent; but there is all the difference in the world between the light and careless manner in which I rapidly move along some pebbly shallow or glassy reach, and the loving care with which I dwell upon the interstices among the rocks, the rippling, moderately strong runs, and other likely spots where instinct and experience tell me that trout are sure to rise. For sport and real fishing give me the river-bank, a clear stage, and no human companion, except perhaps at the midday lunch, until the close of the day.

But I am speaking of sport, and as a fisherman only. If I had not fished in lochs, I should have missed some of the most lovely scenes and enjoyable days I have ever spent. My mind recalls pictures of Loch Awe in the late spring, when the large globe ranunculus is in flower, of island, castle, rock, and wood, and Ben Cruachan towering overhead; of many a smaller tarn sparkling like a jewel among the hills; of the ospreys screaming over Loch Luichart, and of beautiful Colonsay with its three long lochs running straight in from the Atlantic, and Loch Sgoltaire among the hills higher up, with its ruined castle and lovely view of Mull through the cleft in the hills by the Cailleach. Perhaps it may be said that I might have seen all these lochs without fishing them. True enough, O sapient critic; but self-examination compels me to confess that it is most improbable that I should have done so.

CHAPTER XII

GROUSE

WHY is it that there is something in the word "grouse" which raises a thrill in the heart of every sportsman, and of a good many others with little claim to the title? It is certainly not any particular merit the grouse has as a test of the high qualities of the marksman, for I doubt whether any bird—even the hedgerow pheasant beloved by our ancestors—is quite so easy to shoot as a grouse rising to dogs after a steady point on the Twelfth of August. But your grouse has the advantage of the first start. The guns are brought out of "dock," whether they have been resting on the shelves of a dry cupboard or warehoused with a competent and trustworthy gunmaker—for my part I prefer to shift the responsibility for their condition to another, now that it can be so readily done at a small cost—and leaving the counting-house, the Courts, or the House of Commons, you find yourself, after a night in the train—which every year approximates more nearly to the comforts of an hotel—either on board a West Coast steamer enjoying the sea-breezes and the fairyland panorama of the Hebrides, or delivered at your destination, even in Inverness or Sutherland, at a time which would have seemed fabulous to our not very remote progenitors. I remember the late Laird of Poltalloch, who died in 1893, telling me how his father used to ride the whole way from London, purchasing his horse and having his saddle made before starting; and how, having been asked to patronise a young man just starting in business, he gave the first order to the founder of a famous firm still in the front rank of London saddlers and harness-makers. The journey then took three weeks. Now you may go to the theatre in London one evening, and arrive at Poltalloch in time for luncheon on the next day!

Happy is the man who is not obliged to defer his holiday till the last moment before the Twelfth, but can devote a few days to the burn and loch trout, to potting those troublesome rabbits with a pea-rifle, and trying the young pointers and setters over a few of the neighbouring moors. He is not so likely as some to find upon the day his native heath very different from his native flagstones, and to collapse utterly at noon like Mr. Briggs. However, for many it is good fortune enough to be able to begin a holiday on the eve of the happy day, and members of Parliament have usually only been able to obtain even that privilege either by neglect of their duties or the useful institution of a "pair." Still, the flesh is weak, and these are the confessions of one who, while he held a seat in the House, generally contrived to have his feet upon the heather when the blissful Twelfth came round.

Those happy Twelfths! My memory carries me back over thirty years, every autumn of which has been spent in the North. There are few parts of Scotland, from Sutherland to the Border, which have not echoed to the report of my gun. What varieties of scene, what differences of climate, flit across the mind's eye at the thought of the first day of the season; tropical heat, arctic cold, light breezes, and shifting clouds; thunder and lightning and torrents of rain; the round rolling hills of Ross-shire; the Perthshire tablelands, so easy to walk after the hard climb to get to them; the broken mountains of Argyle, with their succession of small hills and valleys and constantly recurring visions of blue sea and distant islands; the down-like Border country, intersected by Esk, Teviot, and Dryfe, and rich with a thousand memories of Christopher North and Sir Walter. Each of these spots has a charm of its own; for Caledonia, like another Queen—

'Governs men by change, and so she sways all moods."

As the blissful date draws round, I feel at peace with all mankind, and disinclined to take a controversial line. Let others exalt the varied charms of driving, shooting over dogs, walking in line, or stalking the old cocks round the hillocks —each method has its uses, each its delights; but let us at least tolerate the idiosyncrasies of others. When I hear a man say that he sees no sport in driving, I find out, in nine cases out of ten, that he is either an indifferent shot or has had little or no experience of what he is denouncing. But I plead for a reciprocal toleration from the driving expert who "fails to see any fun in knocking down slow-flying birds getting up under your feet." A good shot finds plenty of scope for his powers in selecting the right birds, and bringing them down neatly and well; and if the survival of the fittest is to extinguish every breed of sporting dog except the retriever, I hope it will not be in my day. It is delightful to see a pair of well-trained setters or pointers quartering the ground; and if you know and love your dogs, how often their faults and peculiarities rather endear them to you than otherwise!

"He is all fault who has no fault at all," and when Tim or Shuna chases that rabbit which jumps up under his nose, comes back sheepishly for the licking he knows he deserves, exhibits boundless and exuberant joy when he finds how easily he has got off, and repeats the same performance almost before the whip has been pocketed, it is impossible not to laugh, especially if you are not personally responsible for the training of the delinquent. Of one thing I am perfectly convinced—it is not the number of birds killed which constitutes the charm of shooting. My bag has varied from a hundred brace and over to my gun, killed more than once in Forfarshire in the record year 1872, to a few brace shared with a couple of schoolboys; yet it is hard to say which days I have enjoyed most. Of course there are some days and years especially noteworthy. In 1872 the first Lord Cairns, his brother-in-law, Mr. McNeil, dear Edward Ross, the Queen's Prizeman—now also, alas! no more—and myself got over 1500 brace over dogs in ten days; and on August 25, the second time over the ground, I got by myself 75½ brace of grouse and a few snipe and hares; and for contrast, I remember the stormy day when Lord Lauderdale was killed by lightning on the moor, when the wet and cold was so severe in Argyleshire that one of our pointers actually died on the hill then and there from the effect of cold and exposure.

Let the reader now accompany me for a short time to the country I know and love best—dear Argyleshire, where forty brace over dogs is, and always has been, a great day; but which, in spite of all drawbacks of climate, is, in my judgment, the most delightful place in Scotland

Our dogcart has just driven through the

little village of Kilmartin, and we have passed first the old manse and the kirk, and the ancient granite monuments and crosses which represent an earlier form of Christianity, and shortly afterwards the staring Free Church, with "desirable villa residence" adjoining, a little farther on just below the ruins of the old castle of Kilmartin. Another old ruin, that of Carnasary Castle, crowns the hill on the left, for we are at a place where three passes converge; and the Highland chiefs of former days had reasons, not always disinterested, for keeping the highways under their immediate observation. A fair-sized burn—the Scoinish—runs in a straight artificial course close by the side of the road. As a fisherman, I regret that it was not allowed to have its own wilful way; but it is easy to see that if the road was to possess anything but an intermittent existence, the diversion of the stream was a necessity. The old river-course twisting and turning along the valley to the left, with all the varieties of pool and shallow, narrow and rapid, was doubtless much more to the taste of trout and salmon, but floods must have of necessity been frequent and destructive. Now the fishing is not of much account, and an occasional sea-trout after a spate is all it affords to the legitimate angler, although hundreds of salmon run up in the autumn to spawn, and doubtless pay toll to the poacher when out of condition. In the corner under the plantation a deep hole, now dry, still bears the title of the "Pool of the Coat of Mail." Tradition relates that a Maccallum, after a gallant defence of the old castle of Kilmartin against a band of his hereditary foes, was obliged to sally forth when they had set fire to his stronghold and made it literally "too hot to hold him." He succeeded in cutting his way through his tormentors, but had to jump into the pool to cool his armour, which was too warm to be comfortable. Lucky for him that the engineers had not then had their wicked will with the stream, for now the water is hardly knee-deep, and the poor man would have been roasted like a lobster in its shell.

Nothing, it seems, daunts the true disciple of Izaak Walton, for there, in front of us, is one in a deplorable plight. He stands in the road with a rod of portentous length leaning against the dyke beside him. His eyes are turned upwards as if appealing to Heaven; but as we draw nearer we ascertain that he is otherwise occupied, and that the words proceeding out of his mouth are not supplications. His hook is attached to the telegraph wire over his head, half way between the two posts, and, in spite of violent jerks, the stout gut declines to give way. His position tells its own story.

Evidently he has had a bite, and, striking "not wisely but too well," has caught—not the fish, but the telegraph wire. There is nothing for it but a break, for even if he could swarm up one of the posts, the hook would still be out of his reach. We cannot wait to see the finale, but until we turn the corner the connection is still complete.

When we turn again to the right, it is easy enough to see that we are skirting the course of what was once a far mightier stream, but one that has been diverted in prehistoric times and by no human hand. We are now within three miles of Loch Awe, on a nearly level road, and the traces of a large river are clearly visible immediately below us. Under the precipitous wooded hill to our left, great water-worn boulders show where a grand pool must formerly have been, but pheasants and rabbits are feeding where salmon and trout once lurked. Doubtless this was once the course of the River Awe, and there would be no great engineering difficulty in letting the lake run this way again. A little bit farther on, where we turn off the main road, the two small lochs where the wild ducks and coot are feeding, as well as the burn we pass on our way up the brae, discharge their waters into Loch Awe.

The road here degenerates into a mere farm track, very steep in places; but we have not much farther to go, for here is Stroneska farm, where dogs and keepers are waiting for us. Altogether there are eight dogs—six pointers and two setters; but two of the pointers are only young ones in their first season, brought out more for the benefit of their education than to help the sport. In addition to the head-keeper, and the one to whose beat the ground belongs, there are two gillies, one of whom bears on his back an enormous pannier, capable of holding some thirty brace of grouse, and no light weight, if, as occasionally happens, it is filled at the close of the day. It is the theory of the laird that ponies cannot be taken over the ground, and there is no doubt that there are many excessively boggy hollows and awkward dykes; but I confess to being sceptical as to the alleged impossibility, having seen much of the instinctive capacity of a well-trained Highland pony for finding its way across difficult country. However, the gillies do not have a hard time of it. Their duty is to keep out of sight of us, but within sound of a whistle, in case fresh dogs or cartridges are wanted, and most of their time is spent in lounging about until the end of the day's sport, when the hamper has to be taken down to the dog-cart. Then it is a sight to see how a tall Highlander can step out in spite of the weight on his shoulders; but your West Coast man is better at an energetic spurt than at prolonged exertion.

The first part of our beat is up a low hill, mainly grass and rushes, with only a few patches of heather; still, it is worth while to hunt it, as it is on the way, and there is nothing so tiresome as a long walk to the ground. The principal inhabitants are the ubiquitous rabbits, which here and now are a nuisance, and nothing but it. When you see the side of a hill literally alive with them in the late evenings, it is hard to believe that men still living remember the first artificial introduction of the rabbit into Argyleshire, and the prophecies that they would never do in such a wet climate. "Let Rake go!" and off gallops a strong well-proportioned setter, delighted to have the first turn—a distinction he owes rather to his defects than to his merits, as it is now impossible to spoil him. "Is that a very young dog?" says my companion, rather new to the sport and misled by the frantic activity of the débutant. "He is as old as a man," is the reply of the keeper—a slight exaggeration, but bordering on the truth, for I can remember Rake almost as an institution. What a hot day that was at Achoish, when, we having toiled all the morning and found no birds, Rake caught the sheep by the leg! He never was known to do such a thing before or since, and I firmly believe he thought that we ought to have some flesh meat to take home, and that, as it appeared to be hopeless to find grouse, mutton should serve our turn for the nonce. But see—to-day he has turned to stone about a hundred and fifty yards off, and my companion cocks his gun and quickens his pace. I warn him not to hurry, that it is always better to go slow up to a point—a counsel of perfection which he hears but does not obey; and while my judgment condemns, my heart rather approves, for is he not young—lucky fellow!—and this the first point of the season? I have a pretty good notion what Rake has found in that rushy bit, and if I am right there is no hurry.

We get close up to the dog before anything moves, and have to force him forward, so near is he to the game; then there is a whirr of wings, and, just as the warning "'Ware hen" breaks from my lips, there is a report and a fall, and the laws of the country and of sport are outraged by the destruction of a well-grown young grey hen. Alas for the beginning of the season! Yet, let those who have never committed a similar mistake first cast a stone at my companion, who is profuse in his apologies, and sees the old hen and seven other young birds fly off almost in succession, presenting the most tantalising marks. Next, two or three snipe rise one after another,

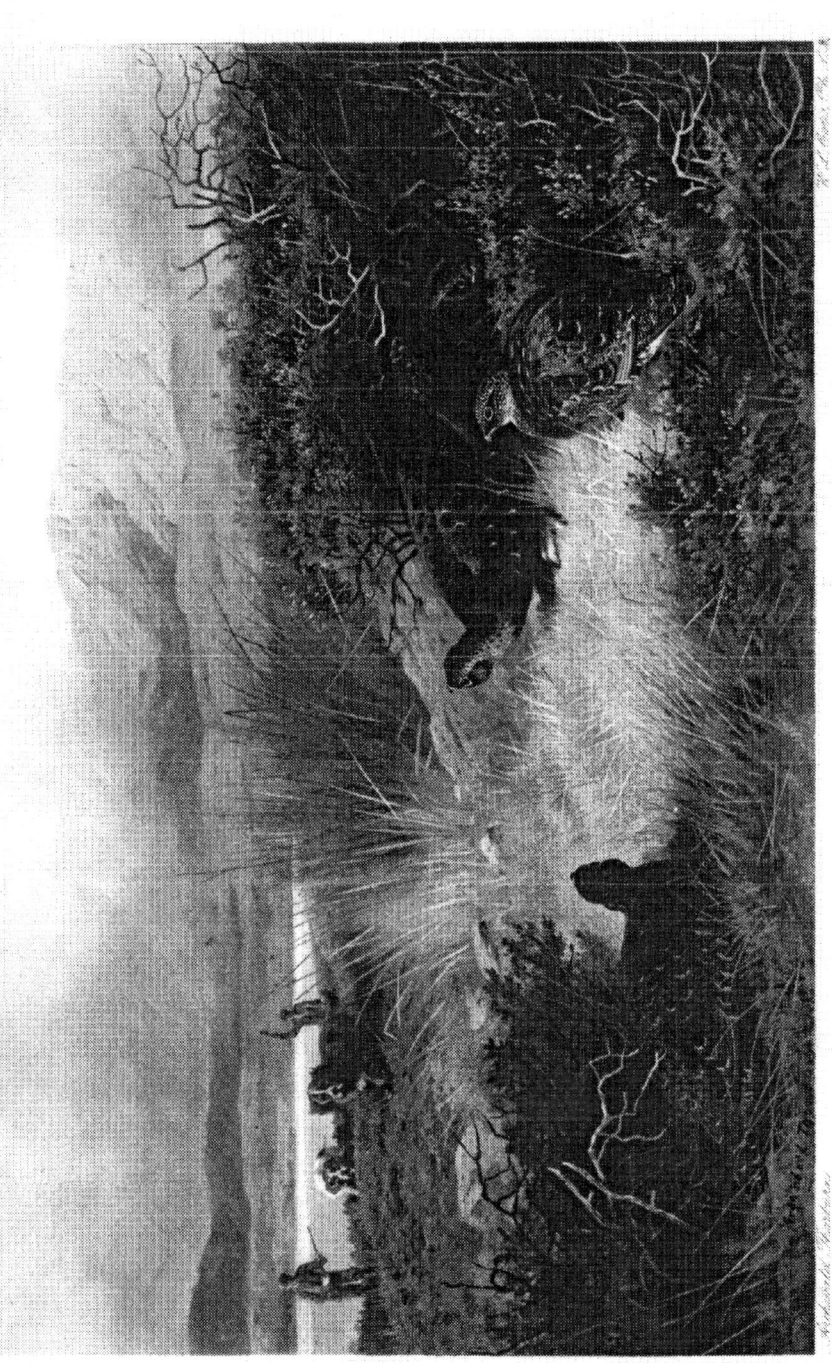

A capital scent.

and a couple of them fall victims, while Rake
—alas! that I should say it—more than once
points at a rabbit, but in a constrained attitude
and with glaring eyes, which gives me a pretty
good idea what he is after. We do not fire
at the rabbits, not merely for fear of spoiling
the dog, but also because if we killed all we
saw the bag would be difficult to carry, and
we are after nobler game. We are now coming
to the heather, and we might safely hunt the
younger dogs, but I cannot find it in my heart
to take Rake up until he has had a chance,
which comes quickly enough. A capital point,
and a nice rise of a good covey of nine; this
time there is no mistake made, and two brace
are neatly killed—one by each gun—the young
birds well grown and feathered. Then we whistle
up the reserve dogs, and Rake is taken up for
the present—a pair of white and tan pointers,
Juno and Diomede, quartering the ground in
front of them with clockwork regularity.

So the morning goes on with varying fortune:
the sun is rather hot, the scent not first-rate,
and sometimes we go half-an-hour without a
shot; but when we reach the wire fence by the
march of Craig-an-terrive, we find that another
sportsman has been on the ground. We pick
up two freshly killed grouse, and from the condition of their heads it is easy to see that the
murder has been the work of a peregrine. Here

the keeper casts a reproachful glance at me, as I never fire my gun at the magnificent birds, and rejoice at the laird's orders that they should not be trapped. Inveterate poachers they are, no doubt—but what a beautiful thing is the swoop of a wild peregrine! Perhaps I shall see my friend himself later on. By one o'clock we stop at a lovely little spring, coming straight out of the side of the hill, and stretch our limbs and inspect the bag while our luncheon is being unpacked. There are eleven brace of grouse—counting the grey hen, which must masquerade under that title, and an old blackcock—whose illegal slaughter must, I fear, be attributed not to accident, but design—four snipe and a hare. Altogether a fair morning's work; for I usually calculate on the afternoon bag doubling that of the morning—the birds are easier to find, and the evening is the best time for shooting. There let them cool while we discuss our lunch and the best pipe of the day.

Half-an-hour—or perhaps three-quarters!—sees us once more on the move, and here we are on some of our best ground, just above Loch Leachan—a fair-sized loch, with a curious little stone island near its middle. It is very calm just now, and although it is some distance off, we can see a flock of duck near the reeds, and the circles made by the rising trout. Here we pick up a good many birds, and spare one or two coveys of squeakers—second broods, to all appearance; and here we fall in with our poacher of the morning. As we round the corner of a knoll, three curlews come flying towards us, and, contrary to the custom of these shy birds, keep going round us in circles, close to the ground and almost within gunshot; and, sure enough, behind them is the falcon, who sheers off when he observes us, but does not go far off, if I know anything of his habits. When, later, the curlews fly off in the direction of Loch Crinan, there is a rush of wings, and we see one of the finest bits of wild hawking it was ever my privilege to witness. I have seen the falcon after terns, ducks, and grouse, but I never saw anything to equal that rapid flight after the curlew —one of which, alas! succumbed at last, but at such a distance that I could only just note that the two joined and fell together.

We now turn in the same direction as the falcon flew, for, like the curlew, our home is by the sea; and at half-past six Duncan and his panniers are despatched by a straight path to Roodel Glen, where the keeper's cart is waiting. He carries nearly thirty brace on his back; and we have added two or three more to the bag, as well as a couple and a half of ducks, by the time we reach the glen at seven o'clock. Happily, the dogcart has been sent for us— a concession to my age and infirmities, as it always used to be the custom to walk home from Roodel. But I am just as well pleased to be spared two miles along the road after a day which has been fairly hard, although thoroughly enjoyable.

CHAPTER XIII

GROUSE-DRIVING

ONE of the most remarkable characteristics of the red grouse is the difference in the degree of wildness which it shows in different localities. In some of the islands on the west coast of Scotland it is difficult to make the coveys rise, even late in the season; and it would be possible for persevering and persistent guns to exterminate the breed altogether. On the mainland of Argyleshire, and especially in the south of the peninsula of Cantyre, the grouse are still very tame during the early part of the season, and even late in October will often sit to dogs on a fine day with bright sun and a slight touch of frost. In Perthshire early good sport can be had with pointers and setters, although several coveys rise out of range, but later in the season it is next to impossible to approach the birds, except round the corners of hills, or in very broken ground, and dogs are rather a hindrance than a help. A single very steady old pointer or setter, or a well-broken spaniel which will keep quite close to hand, will sometimes find a stray bird so unaccountably tame that otherwise it would have escaped notice; but this is the exception which proves the rule. Coming farther south to the Border country, on the long rolling moors of Eskdale and Teviotdale the grouse are still wilder, and I have the dogs taken up and walking in line resorted to for preference, even in the first week in August. In Westmorland the birds are wilder than in Roxburghshire and Berwick, and in many parts of Yorkshire the practice of walking after grouse at all has fallen quite into desuetude—a strange anomaly, which cannot altogether be accounted for by the character of the heather and the number of birds. It is true, as a rule, that birds are wildest where they are most plentiful and where the heather is shortest; but I have known them tame on very bare ground and unapproachable in the most luxuriant heather, and it really seems as if the nature of the birds varied in different localities. The practice of driving has its origin, not in the laziness of the modern sportsman, but in the necessity for some method of getting at birds which had really learnt to defy all other modes of pursuit. For this purpose the wildness of the birds is actually an advantage. Fewer beaters are required to put them up and send them forward, and the tame coveys, which alight before facing the line of fire, and run about spying the ground before them with outstretched necks and uplifted heads, are almost certain to penetrate the secret of the most skilful ambush, and to face the waving flags and demonstrative gestures of beaters and flankers in preference to the hidden danger indicated by the glint of a barrel or the motion of a hand. What originated in necessity has been continued from choice, and from its own inherent advantages. Wherever driving has been adopted, grouse have increased in numbers and in health, as the old cocks have found their tactics of getting off in advance of their juvenile relations resulted in their drawing the first fire instead of escaping altogether. Gradually the practice spread, and the inveterate conservatism of keepers has at length, and with difficulty, been induced to tolerate, and eventually encourage, driving with the best results, in places where for years they asserted that it was impossible and absurd to attempt it.

I do not wish to embark upon the well-worn controversy, carried on not so much between the actual votaries of driving and shooting over dogs, as between certain writers masquerading in their names, whose works usually betray an equal ignorance of both methods. My tastes are catholic in such matters, and it does not seem necessary to exalt one sport by disparaging another. I should be very sorry to see shooting over dogs altogether done away with, for nothing in my eyes is more beautiful than to see a pair of well-trained pointers or setters ranging a moor obedient to the least gesture or motion of a *silent* keeper. I would as soon see horses altogether displaced by puffing and smelling automobiles, as lose my opportunity of watching those beautiful examples of instinct and training; but it is not necessary to shut one's eye to certain obvious advantages of driving, or to declaim against "arm-chair" sportsmen. It is idle to deny that a driven grouse presents a much more difficult mark for the gun than a bird rising just when you expect him in the very spot indicated by a point. The "proof of the pudding is in the eating," and numbers of men can secure a good bag walking who can hardly kill one bird out of twenty streaming over their heads. It is a real treat to see a first-rate workman crumple up his birds, but it requires long training as well as a quick hand and eye before two guns can be so handled as to enable the owner to secure three or four birds out of a pack. Again, driving is a more sociable form of sport than its rival, and the same ground will provide amusement for a large party. But I love variety; and the ideal moor to my thinking is one where the birds sit well to dogs early in the season, and the drivers get their turn later on.

For a detailed and scientific description of

all the best ways and means of carrying on a drive successfully, I must refer my readers to the admirable articles by Lord Granby, published in the "Badminton," and to the well-known treatise of Mr. Archibald Stuart Wortley on "Grouse" in the "Fur, Feather, and Fin" series. Both are past masters of the art upon which they write, and are as skilful with the pen as with the double-barrel. A keeper who can manage a drive well is a treasure, and requires all the qualities of a general commanding an army in the field—temper, patience, and influence over men as well as an accuracy of observation and instinctive knowledge of the habits of birds and animals. The conformation of the ground and the currents of the wind should also be thoroughly noted, and, given a combination of knowledge and these qualities, there is hardly any place where I should pronounce successful driving to be impossible. The position of the butts must of course be determined by the trend of the ground; but they should be placed in as straight a line as possible, and so concealed from the front by rising ground that the guns can get into their places, having approached them unseen. The rising ground should, however, not be too near, as it is next to impossible to shoot well if you are unable to see your birds until they are close upon you. This combination of advantages cannot, however, be obtained in all instances, and one or more of the guns has to put up with very difficult shots, but is often compensated for his disadvantage in that respect by getting more birds over him than those who are favoured with a more distant horizon. The sides of the butts should be sufficiently high to screen the occupant from chance pellets, but this again is not always possible, and great care should be exercised not to fire along the line. This may sound like an unnecessary warning, or one, at all events, that should only be addressed to tailors and tyros; but my experience shows that it needs to be hammered in by constant repetition. I have seen good and careful sportsmen, new to grouse-driving, fire dangerous shots, and have had difficulty afterwards in persuading them of the truth of the impeachment. The fact is that they believed that they were firing well in front, and did not allow for the swing of the gun in following the bird at an obtuse angle to the right or left. The safe rule is only to shoot birds either well in front or behind, and never under any circumstances to follow the pack with the barrels right round a semicircle. Different treatment is meted out to delinquents by different people. I remember one sufferer whom I found bleeding from a wound in the nose at the end of a drive, who entreated me to say nothing about it, as he was sure his next-door neighbour would be dreadfully unhappy if he knew he had hit him; and another, less indulgent, who placed a careless sportsman in a gravel-pit for the remainder of the day, patiently expecting the grouse, which were being driven in quite a different direction.

The careful placing of flankers is even of more importance than the regulation of the drivers themselves. A pack is readily turned by a concealed flag-bearer rising at the right moment, the element of surprise and suddenness being more important for the purpose of alarming wild creatures than any obtrusive and noisy demonstrations. The drivers themselves should advance in a good military line and at an even pace, holding their flags in an upright position. They should preserve silence, and not trouble themselves to shout and wave their flags at birds flying back. Such tactics only very occasionally turn a covey which has made up its mind to "face the music," and are decidedly detrimental to the general success of the drive. I have often contrasted the mechanical advance of a well-drilled team, say in Yorkshire or the Lowlands, with the antics of the scratch pack who are pressed together for an occasional drive in Argyleshire. The latter is very amusing, but it is not the real article. The line is erratic, and the moment a covey rises, all the beaters stand still waving flags and shouting "Mark!" until they are out of sight. As a consequence, the birds a long way ahead become on the alert, and often have grasped the fact that a drive is going on in time to give mature consideration to their safest line of flight. Probably, however, if your sense of humour is keen, you may derive so much amusement from the performance of your ill-disciplined assistants as will compensate you for the loss of a certain amount of sport.

It is well to be prepared for all weathers, more especially for extremes of cold and heat. A good warm cape, which can be easily thrown off when the birds begin to come, is an almost indispensable requisite; and a good tweed is preferable to a waterproof, and will turn almost as much wet. It is a risky thing to sit facing a bleak north-easter or a West Highland shower in thin garments, after you have heated yourself with a climb, often long and severe, to get from one set of butts to another. I think I have been colder out driving than when pursuing any other form of sport. Spring fishing on the Tay, or waiting for the mist to clear in an exposed place in a deer-forest, are chilly proceedings, but a snowstorm in November accompanied by a cold squall is also a very effective method of reducing the temperature. One sportsman, a member of Parliament, was guilty of the heinous crime of lighting a fire in his butt and going to sleep, letting the grouse stream over his head uninjured; and extenuating circumstances may at least be pleaded in mitigation of his sentence. I have started out grouse-driving on worse days than I have ever faced any other form of shooting. It is difficult to say No when a drive has been planned long beforehand and guns and beaters collected from a distance, especially when the end of the season is approaching and it must be now or never. The best way is to be prepared to face all contingencies, and remember that often a very bad morning ripens out into a bright day, while determined bad weather may follow on the most glorious sunrise. It is not like covert-shooting, where a really wet morning is fatal to sport, as the undergrowth will be dripping and the birds draggled, even if the weather clears soon after the start; for grouse soon recover the effects of the heaviest showers, and rise more easily and fly farther after some hours of storm. The views too after the air has cleared are often magnificent, and as I write I can recall glorious views of Ailsa Craig and Arran from the rolling hills of Ayrshire, or the mist clearing from the high hills around Millden or Invermark.

An improvised drive, when birds have turned out too wild to walk, or a lot of old blackcocks or grouse have been spied on a hillside stubble or a green brae on the edge of a moor, is also very amusing. It is a real triumph to circumvent the former—wily old stagers with lyre-shaped tails and glossy plumage, which always rise well out of shot unless stalked or driven. How the heart beats as one cautiously crawls round under peat hag or dyke, and what excitement one has for a too brief quarter of an hour or twenty minutes, from the first peep, when one finds that one has gained one's ambush unperceived. Next, uplifted heads and excited movements show that the birds have detected the advance of the keepers and gillies before you can see any of them, and then all take to flight, perhaps disappointing you by going right away to the right or left, but sometimes coming straight over you, and leaving two of their number dead, before and behind you. Such a shot is worth a dozen on a set day, for you feel that you have pitted your own instinct and experience against that of those sagacious creatures, and come off the conqueror.

CHAPTER XIV

CHILL OCTOBER

A FINE crisp morning, with a touch of white frost on the ground. What is to be the order of the day? The river will not fish, as there has been no rain to speak of for the last three days, and the tide will be in the lower pools; so we must go into the gunroom and consult Robert Brodie, the keeper.

What a typical snuggery was the old gunroom at Poltalloch!—the cedar cupboards containing every variety of weapon in use during the past forty years, representing the progress of arms of precision from ancient muzzle-loading guns and rifles to the latest hammerless ejectors and expresses; and of fishing-rods and reels, from weather-beaten hickory joints and weird multiplying brass winches with huge projecting handles, to the latest triumph of the most celebrated London, Alnwick, or Irish makers.

In the centre of the mantelpiece hangs a trophy from Canada—a huge moose's head, with each flat horn big enough to make a comfortable seat, back and all; while underneath it is a strange nondescript, so singed by a hundred candles that, were it not for the claws on the shield beside it, it would be difficult to recognise it for the "old man" kangaroo which turned desperately to bay after a sharp breather in South Australia. At the far end, African antelopes' horns surmount a trophy of South Sea clubs, which have an historical interest as well as a decorative value, for they were a gift from Captain Cook to his friend Dr. Orme—the great-grandfather of the present laird—presented just before he sailed on his last fatal voyage on July 11, 1776. In the corner are a confused bundle of old bows and arrows, a narwhal horn, and the weapon of a swordfish; while above the cupboard two miserable little red deers' heads from the island of Jura testify by contrast to the care with which the breed has been improved by Mr. Evans, the present lessee of the forest, to enable him to show the splendid trophies which now decorate his dining-room walls. How many a jolly evening have I spent in that dear old gunroom! What pleasant companions used to gather there for their sociable cigars and pipes—seated, some of them, on cartridge boxes and cane chairs; for the old prejudice against a regular smoking-room still existed. As I write, I still seem to sniff the scent of the cocoanut matting and to hear the drip of the rain from the eaves into the balcony outside—a welcome sound, as it meant a spate and the river in order before long.

A ring at the bell, and old Brodie's slow step is heard approaching along the passage—a slow step now, for he is old and "gey stout;" but in his day there was not a better walker or a keener hand. His time on the hill is over, and now he reserves himself for a general superintendence; but what he especially loves is driving his cart along the roads when we are hunting the woods for fallow deer, "for fear they should break oot." How often has the tootle of his horn announced that the buck has evaded us, in spite of the wheels of his chariot!

After a good deal of shouting—for old Robert is very hard of hearing, and, like many deaf persons, thinks it necessary to raise his voice, as if everybody shared his infirmity—it is arranged that Brock and I should try for a mixed bag along the river, and finish up the day by waiting under the bank of the burn in the evening between the brae face of Achnashellach and the field of oats near the river, which are not yet carried, when we may hope to get some nice rocketing shots at grouse and blackcock coming in to feed. No need to go on wheels; we can start from opposite the kennels, and have the dogcart to meet us at Bridge End in the evening. And at half-past ten we duly rendezvous at the gate by the Scoinish burn, where the keeper and two gillies are waiting with an old steady pointer — and York, the antediluvian retriever. We take our guns at once; for there are a couple of fields of scanty turnips and potatoes between the moss and the burn, where we may find a covey of partridges to vary the bag. We mean to get at least eight sorts of game to-day; and, if lucky, we may easily do better, for I have often seen many more than that number of varieties on the ground we are to traverse in the next few hours.

We shall not long be left in doubt, for the old dog will cover the whole field in a few minutes, and, sure enough, he is feeling something now. A whirr of wings, and I just stop myself in time from pulling the trigger at a half-grown hen-pheasant, and a minute or two later five partridges rise and sweep to the left across my companion, who neatly disposes of a brace. First blood for Harry! We now come to a little heathery fir plantation intersected by the road to Drimvawr. Here we go forward while it is carefully beaten through, as it almost always holds game. A fine old cock-pheasant blunders up just opposite to me, and I stop his course through the fir trees. His long spurs tell of many a year's race across the moor, and he evidently would not have risen —for there are no such refinements as stops— had he not, unfortunately for himself, shaped his course direct for my feet. We are in luck here this morning, as we get two glossy old blackcocks, a pigeon, and a woodcock—probably one bred on the ground, as the flights from abroad do not begin to arrive until about the full moon on the 10th at earliest. Three roe are seen, one a buck with a pretty head; but although we should like to add another specimen to the bag, we neither of us care to shoot at them with a smooth-bore.

A few steps onwards bring us, past a small cluster of old "black houses," to the foot-bridge across the Add, near Dalnahassaig. As we cross it, the river looks deceptively high, but there is a deadness of the current and an oily smoothness out of the wind which reveal to the practised eye that the tide is in. A red fish—a soldier—greets us with a splash as we pass; but we pay him no attention, as we are not having what we call a "Robinson Crusoe day" to-day. Sometimes I have visited these happy hunting-grounds with a gun, a rod, and a pea-rifle, so as to be ready to stalk a blackcock on the peat stacks with the latter weapon, or to get a duck, snipe, or plover, or grouse on the edge of the moor in the intervals of flogging the pools for salmon and sea-trout; and my boys used to call such days "Robinson Crusoe days," from my fancied resemblance to the old pictures of the solitary islander parading his little kingdom with his fine assortment of weapons.

But what are those little brownish birds running about so busily beyond the cattle on the green rushy field immediately opposite the end of the bridge? Golden plovers, but in a perfectly bare open place, where there is no chance of stalking them. Still something must be attempted to secure so acceptable an addition to the bag and the larder; and after some discussion, it is settled that Harry shall creep round under the broken bank of the river, and hide himself just where there is a white gate in the iron fence, while one of the gillies stands on the bridge as a "flanker," and I and the others go round and try to drive them—not an easy thing to do, for they generally go where they wish, irrespective of your desires in the matter. However, an unusual, although by no means unprecedented, thing happens on this occasion. Generally these very shy birds are off with a shrill whistle long before you are within a hundred yards of them; but occasionally they have a stupid fit, and it is with surprise that I find myself within fifty and then forty yards before they take flight. Then, just as I am trying to get two or three in line, for no law is given to these migrants, they rise, and I fire one barrel at that moment and another as, with a rapid turn of the wings, altering the shape and position of the flock, they pass rather wide to the right. Two fall at once, one a runner, and another drops a hundred yards off. No very suc-

The old moor.

cessful result, as I have often known more to fall to one shot, but the number killed at a fairly long range is rather a matter of luck than skill; and nothing comes of the ambuscade, as the flock disappears out of sight without giving my companion a chance.

Just beyond the bend of the stream is a considerable-sized swampy patch of reeds known as the "old river," doubtless a former bed of the Add, which has changed its course in more than one place for natural and artificial reasons, almost within living memory. This is a certain find for snipe, and must be carefully worked; so we walk along, one on each side, with the keeper between us, but not in the middle, as it would in places take him nearly over his head; while the old retriever splashes about in the centre, as if he understood and enjoyed the job—as is, indeed, the case. We have put No. 8 cartridges in the right-hand barrel, but kept our No. 5 in the left, as there may be a stray duck or some teal left, although a large flock of the former flew away when the double shot was fired at the plovers. It is wet, and tiresome walking, and none the more pleasant that the snipe seem to be wild to-day. Half a dozen are "scape scaping" out of range of us before we have well settled to business, and the first and second shots are fruitless of result, and perhaps ought not to have been fired at all, as the birds were almost, if not quite, out of range. But the next bird rises quite close to my feet, and there was no excuse for my missing him, as I did, except flurry and the provoking irregularity of his flight. However, the next two fall, and we do pretty well along the remainder of the beat, securing altogether five couple and a half, a duck, and two teal. Six of these little beauties rose within shot of Harry, and he ought to have got a right and left, but only secured one; however, he retrieved his laurels by killing the second stone dead, as the bereaved five wheeled round a second time almost out of shot.

There is not likely to be much in the rushy field between us and Dunadd, the hill about a mile beyond us. There may be a hare or an odd snipe or so; but we look about us and note the flock of old blackcocks that are nearly always sitting on the edge of the moss somewhere hereabouts, but are too wary to often pay toll to the sportsman. If we tried to stalk them, the chances are that after one of us had had a long crawl in a damp drain they would be off just as he was hoping against hope for a shot, and settle again to jeer at us not far off—very likely on the bank of the "old river" we have just left.

"A blot in heaven, the raven flying high,"

whose unmistakable bark calls attention to his presence, is all we see afterwards until we arrive at Dunadd, where we intend to stop for lunch.

Dunadd is a queer-shaped solitary hill rising out of the flat moss, and a keeper stationed there with a good glass can spy a poacher on any pool in the river from Kilmichael to Crinan, which accounts for the fact that unlawful rod-fishing by day is a form of poaching seldom attempted. At its foot, in a snug little recess under a rock overgrown with lastræa and lady-fern, a beautiful little ice-cold spring marks an ideal halting-place; and as it is the only well for some miles, and close to a first-rate stretch of the river, luncheon is so often served there between one and two that, but for our tidy habit of burning our paper when we light our pipes, the grass around it would resemble the Green Park after a Bank Holiday. There the game is laid out, and we dispose of half a cold grouse, some bread-and-butter, egg sandwiches with a little cress in them, and a slice of cake, washed down with the cool spring water just flavoured with the Lovat blend. A salmon from time to time splashes in the pool below, and we can see the light form of a fallow deer feeding on the rocky clearing in Ballimore wood opposite to us, and a pair of buzzards wheeling in broad circles round the summit of Succoth. But we must be stirring soon if we are to be at Achnashellach in time for the blackcock, and somewhat reluctantly we rise from our comfortable seats, and pursue our course up the stream.

We must "gang warily" through the hazel copse at the next bend, as the round backwater just below the Boy's pool is always a sure find for duck, and it is an easy place to get at them. Some rabbits scuttle away through the ferns, and a wood-pigeon flaps round the rowan; but we reserve our fire, and it is lucky that we do so, for eight or nine ducks rise quacking as our heads appear over the dyke, and three of them fall to our volley. A couple of snipe rise as the old dog splashes into the water after the winged mallard; but we have not got our cartridges in quick enough to secure them. A rabbit or two are rolled over as we plod through the rushes; they have an unaccountable love of burrowing in the banks of the river, although numbers are drowned whenever there is a very high flood. My little terrier generally spends the day hunting them when I am after the grilse, but he is very wary of scratching at their holes since the day he got caught in a gin; and if I see him dancing about outside an earth, and giving a series of growls, I can be pretty sure that I shall find a trap there. To-day, however, we are not after bunnies, and content ourselves with just a couple to vary the bag.

Another little marsh near the Stance pool,

and a stony place between two burns for which they have an unaccountable fondness, yield us a few more snipe, and we are at Kilmichael bridge; and, as we walk through the farmyard of Achnashellach, we can see that some at least of the grouse and blackgame are already feeding on the stooks of oats in the field by the river, while more are collected on the rock among the heather, and on the green patches on the brae face. The little burn fortunately flows here between steep banks in a sort of gully, and we can easily crawl to our places unperceived. It is a picked place for the sport. Birds just settling to feed generally fly low and slow, and afford an unsatisfactory mark; but here our ambuscade is in a narrow place, not in the field itself, but halfway between the high hill and the corn, and they come beautifully high down the wind. The keeper is to give us ten minutes law, and then walk through the field and put up what birds are already there, and then concealing himself when this has been done in the plantation beyond, to watch where the birds fall. We have about an hour till dusk, and as we take up our positions some eighty yards apart, we can hear the crowing of the cock grouse on the edge of the moor, and see several old blackcocks walking about on the sky-line, preening their glossy feathers, and showing a little of the white under their tails. A whistle from Neill tells that the birds are up, and soon a stream of more than a hundred are passing over our heads, but rather wide, and then a few stragglers. Harry accounts for three; I only get one with my two barrels, shooting a little behind the first bird through not allowing enough for the pace. The old cocks on the hill take not the slightest notice of the fusillade. They are some distance off, and it is noticeable how little attention these birds pay to the sound of a shot, if the sportsman who fires it keeps out of sight. Soon a sentinel rises from the ground and heads straight for my companion. Now, let me see if he holds forward enough. They go so fast, and look as if they were travelling so slow, that it is easy enough to shoot behind them, and a few pellets too far back have no more apparent effect than a pea-shooter would produce on a tiger. But Harry is not new to the game, and the old sultan crumples up in the air and comes to the ground with a thud.

Another, then a flock, then some grouse. This afternoon we are in luck, and for a short time the fun is fast and furious. Sometimes the old stagers go on unmoved, although the shot can be heard to rattle against their breasts; but there they are well protected by the close feathers, and it really requires No. 4 to make sure of them. One drawback to our amusement is that the wind has dropped altogether, and that the "usual evening midge" is persevering and troublesome, facing the protective tobacco-smoke with a courage worthy of a better cause. But all good things must come to an end, and at last it is time to gather and count the slain, and wend our way to the dogcart waiting on the bridge.

The bags are emptied and the game arranged by the side of the road, and make a picture which Weenix or Snyders would have loved to paint; only there are none of the green woodpeckers, chaffinches, and such like, for which either the artist or the sportsman, or both, used to be responsible. Nine and a half couple of snipe, five ducks, two teal, one woodcock, one pheasant, three partridges, two rabbits, seventeen grouse, twelve blackcocks, and three golden plovers— total, sixty-five head and ten varieties. And as we drive home, well wrapped up, through the now frosty evening air, we agree that, although neither of us despises a good day's cover shooting, such a mixed bag is worth a hecatomb of pheasants.

INDEX

A DAY with a seal, 87-102
Add, river, 8, 136-163
Aflalo, Mr., cost of sport, 3
Anemone, cloak, 115
    ,, plumose, 8
'Antiquary," Sir Walter Scott's, 75
Askew, Mr., introduced rabbits, 13
Awe, Loch, 184
  ,, river, old course of, 193

BADGER, 15
Bag, good mixed, 223
Bird's-foot starfish, 139
Blackcocks, 33, 215, 216
    ,, on stooks, 221
Braemore, 66
Brown, Harvie, "Fauna of Argyll and the Inner Hebrides," 20
Brown snipe, 19

CALDECOTT, Randolph, "Three Jovial Huntsmen," 35
Captain Cook, 212
Cat, wild, 10
Cave for seals near Valentia, Ireland, 75
Chill October, 211-223
Chough, 18
Cloak anemone, 115
Clubs, Captain Cook's, 212
Comatula, 132

Cooking roe, 56
Cormorants, 24
Corvidæ, 18
Cost of sport, Aflalo on, 3
Crinan moss, 7
Crab, hermit, 115
  ,, spider, 115
  ,, swimming, 114
Curlew, 177-198

DALHOUSIE, Lord, 58
Darwin, voyage of the *Beagle,* 121
Day with grilse, a, 163-175
Death of deer, 70
Death of seal, 79, 85
Deer, fallow, at home, 22-41; weight of, 36
  ,, forest, Braemore, 66
  ,, ,, Invermark, 57
  ,, pony, curious accident to, 71
  ,, missed, 63
  ,, roe, chasing the, 41-56
  ,, ,, cooking of, 56
  ,, ,, hunting, 40, 41
  ,, ,, hounds for, 46, 48, 54
  ,, ,, rifle or shot-gun for, 45, 46
  ,, ,, sanctuary for, 55
  ,, ,, tame, 44
  ,, ,, unwounded, killed with knife, 55
  ,, stalking, 57-71
  ,, to rise, waiting for, 65

Depths, out of the, 103-135
Doris, 131
Dr. Orme, 212
Dredging, 103-135
Drive, improvised, 209
Driving grouse, 201-210
Drought of 1894, 153

EAGLE, golden, 15, 16
„ osprey, 16
„ owl, 17
„ sea, 16, 17
Eider duck, 26
Eolis, 131
Evans, Mr. Henry, 212
Esk, North, in flood, 58

FALCON, peregrine, 18, 165, 198
Fallow-deer at home, 20-41
„ „ weight of, 36
"Fauna of Argyll and the Inner Hebrides," by Harvie Brown, 20
Fern, film, 39
„ osmunda, 39
Fiddlers, velvet, 114
Fish, sense of feeling in, 150
Fowler, Sir John, 66
Foxes, number killed, 15
Foxhounds, 26
Freaks, 20

GAFFING salmon, 169
Goat Island, Loch Craignish, 76
Golden eagle, 15, 16
Golden plover, 216
Golf, 90
Grey hen, 196
Grey phalarope, 19
Grilse, a day with the, 163-175
Grouse, bags of, 190
„ day's shooting of, 190-200

Grouse, driving, 201-210
„ killed by falcon, 197
„ shooting, 186-210
„ shooting over dogs, 189
„ „ on stooks, 221
„ variety in wildness of, 201, 202

HARRIERS, 26
Harvie Brown, "Fauna of Argyll," 20
Hawking curlew, 198
Hawks, 18
Hare, sea, 131
Herds of Proteus, the, 72-86
Hermit crab, 115
Hounds for roe, 46, 48
„ „ otter, 54
Hymenophyllum Wilsoni, 39

INTRODUCTION of rabbits, 13
Invermark Forest, 57
Irishman's pool, 146
„ „ netted, 147

JACKDAW, 18
John Fowler, Sir, 66

KINGCUPS, 177
King Harry's shells, 114

LIGHT TACKLE, 161
Loch Awe, 184
„ na-Larich, 176-185
„ Luichart, 185
„ Sgoltaire, 185
„ fishing, 176-185
Lubbock, Alfred, on wild cat 10, 11
Lydekker on wild cat, 10
Lythe, 8

INDEX

Macroramphus griseus, 19
Marten, pine, 11, 12
„ „ St. John's description of, 12
Merganser, 25
Methods of poaching, 147
Midges, 28, 38
Minard Castle, 13
Mixed shooting, 211-223

NIL desperandum, 153-162

OCTOBER, chill, 211-223
Orme, Dr., 212
Osmunda regalis, 39, 40
Osprey, 16
Otter, 15
Out of the depths, 103-135

PARTRIDGES, 214
Pen, sea, 120-125
Pennatula phosphorea, 120, 123
Peregrine falcon, 18, 165, 198
Phalarope, grey, 19
Pheasant, 214
Pigeon, wood, 215
Plover, golden, 216
Proteus, the Herds of, 72-86
Poltalloch, 1-21

RABBITS, 12, 13, 14, 15
Rats, 3, 45
Raven, 218
Redbreasted snipe, 19
Retriever, 26
"Rhyme of the Three Sealers," Kipling's, 73
Roe, 31
„ chasing the, 41-56
„ cooking of, 56
„ hounds for, 46, 48
„ rifle or shot-gun for, 46

Roe, tame, 44
„ unwounded, killed with knife, 55
Rook with deformed beak, 20
Ross, Edward, 58
Ross, Horatio, 58

SABELLA, 131
Salmon-fishing, 136-175
„ good bag of, in low water, 160
Salmon, small flies for, 161, 162
Salmon, wounded by seal, 150
Sea-eagle, 16, 17
„ hare, 120
„ pen, 120, 125
„ rope, 124
„ rush, 106, 117-124
Seal, a day with a, 87-102
„ the Herds of Proteus, 72-86
Seal, at salmon nets, 76
„ cave, 75
„ death of, 79, 85
„ frightened by salute, 79
„ importation of, 72
„ lost, 100
„ on rocks, 92
„ skinning, 101
„ stalking, 92-97
„ uses of, 74
Serpulæ, 130
Sgoltaire, Loch, 185
Smuggling, 9
Snipe, brown, 19
„ redbreasted, 19
„ shooting, 217
Snowy owl, 17, 18

TEAL, 218
Terrier, Poltalloch, 26
Trout, 179, 180, 181

VELVET FIDDLERS, 114
Virgularia mirabilis, 106, 117–124

WATER RANUNCULUS, 177
White woodcock, 20
Wild cat, 10

Wild cat, Lydekker on, 10
,, Alfred Lubbock kills with a stone, 10, 11
Wild duck, 177
,, turkey, 29, 30
Woodcock, 215
,, carrying young, 39
,, white, 20

THE END

Printed by BALLANTYNE, HANSON & Co.
Edinburgh & London